"In an age of ever increasing fickleness and lack of focus, *The Grass Is Browner on the Other Side* is a timely journey that brings us back to the fundamental path to becoming an elite salesperson. Jon Markwardt is a powerhouse salesperson and a world-class sales leader. He is able to combine real-world business experience with an inspiring travel tale to show us there are lessons around us everyday; whether at our desks or jumping off cliffs. This is a book that every salesperson should have on their shelf."

—Steven Weidman, SVP of Sales at ZOZI

"*The Grass Is Browner on the Other Side* is an absolute must-read for anyone in sales. This book is told in a unique and engaging way, providing strong applications to key sales methodologies that will elevate any sales professional to new levels of success. As the lead trainer of a large company, I'd highly recommend this book to anyone in and outside our organization."

—Tom Riley, Senior Manager of Training, Fortune 1000 Company

"There are no bigger sales calls than those made by police officers. I know this well and was able to relate to having a sales position by reading this book. During this time in America, *The Grass Is Browner on the Other Side* should be a must read for everyone wearing the blue."

—Brendan Bligh, Police Officer Northern California

"I've worked for Jon at two different Fortune 1000 companies. His book portrays sales concepts in an entertaining fashion that have become a part of my day-to-day business and have dramatically affected my career. I'm honored to be one of his many success stories!"

—Crystal Cozad, Fortune 1000 Sales Professional

"Whether your goal is to be the top agent in real estate sales or to climb Mount Everest, *The Grass Is Browner on the Other Side* will encourage you to keep your chin up and amplify all of the opportunities around you. Cheers to Jon for penning a positive guide to becoming your best-selling self."

—April Kelly, Entrepreneur,
Author of *Gratitude at Work* and *Spaghetti on the Wall*

"If you want successful transformation in business and in life, *The Grass Is Browner on the Other Side* teaches us that success is an inside job. You will learn to improve your mindset, develop your skillset, and be given the right tools to propel you towards your dreams, aspirations, and goals. Jon will help you get there faster and better than anyone I know."

—Miguel A. de Jesus, Western Area VP Sales
& Regional Manager Paychex, Inc. (Retired),
Speaker, Author, Coach, Transformational Change
Agent & Facilitator, Instructor of Emotional Intelligence

"I was able to identify with numerous concepts in this book that are already assisting me in my profession. As a pediatric ICU nurse, I am constantly having to sell parents on trusting me with the care of their child. I am grateful that this book has taught me new ways to improve my ability to make this sale, which in turn improves the care of the child and the well-being of the parents."

—Jessica Montgomery, Registered Nurse

"There is a reason why elite athletes still need to report for training camp before each season. They need ongoing reinforcement of the very fundamentals that make them successful, while adding updates to their playbook to stay current with new trends. *The Grass Is Browner on the Other Side* is the elite sales professional's playbook for today. This book will provide sales professionals with fundamentals and updates to elevate their sales careers to new heights."

—Tom Zgainer
CEO, America's Best 401k

How to Grow into an Elite Sales Professional

The Grass Is Browner on the Other Side

▶ **SALES EDITION** ◀

JON MARKWARDT

SAN FRANCISCO

THE GRASS IS BROWNER ON THE OTHER SIDE ®

©2017, 2019 Jon Markwardt, Grass Is Browner LLC. All rights reserved. No part of this book may be used or reproduced in any manner whatsoever without written permission except in the case of brief quotations embodied in critical articles or reviews.

Neither the publisher nor the author is engaged in rendering legal or other professional services through this book. If expert assistance is required, the services of an appropriate competent professional should be sought. The author and publisher shall have neither liability nor responsibility to any person or entity with respect to any loss or damage caused, or alleged to have been caused, directly or indirectly by the information contained in this book. Some names and details have been changed within the context of the stories to protect the privacy of the individuals being discussed.

Inquiries: www.GrassIsBrowner.com

Library of Congress Control Number: 2016949207

Cataloging in Publication Data on file with Publisher

Hardcover ISBN: 978-0-9978580-1-3

Paperback ISBN: 978-0-9978580-0-6

Kindle ISBN: 978-0-9978580-2-0

Illustrated by Penelope Constantinou, Nicosia, Cyprus, www.penelope-art.net

Publishing and Production: Concierge Marketing Inc., Omaha, Nebraska

Printed in the United States of America

10 9 8 7 6 5 4 3

To Ken Markwardt

My grandfather once told me when making a career decision to do two things:

1. Calculate your worst-case scenario and determine if you are fine with the result.
2. Look at your personal life and decide if the timing is right.

Upon telling my grandfather that I wanted to write a book on how to become elite in sales, he challenged me on who would read it. My grandfather provided me with my worst-case scenario, and I was fine with it. It is possible that only my closest friends and family members will read this book. The concept of writing this book and having just one person grow their career and become an elite sales professional was all I needed. The right timing in my life provided me with the opportunity to dedicate this book to my grandfather. I thank him for providing me with the confidence to expand my sales career as an author.

Contents

The Traveling Salesman 1

   1. The Magic Sales Potion 7
   2. A Bed For My Backpack 15
   3. Crying Creates Obligation 29
   4. If You're Not Getting Better, You're Dead 51
   5. You Jump, I Jump 71
   6. Building Your Referral Army 83
   7. Just Say No 99
   8. The Front Line of Your Referral Army 115
   9. Your Fallen Soldiers 129
  10. The Negotiation Battle 145
  11. The Sales Science Experiment 169
  12. You Are Legend 183
  13. The Ice Cream Man 193
  14. ABN: Always Be Networking 209
  15. Grow Your Author's Beard 223
  16. Three, Two, One, Fun! 235
  17. Your Grass Is Green 247

Acknowledgments 251
About the Author 255

The Traveling Salesman

The cabin lights are off. Most of the people on my flight are sleeping. Some are watching movies. The lady in front of me is reading a gossip magazine. And before I catch some rest, I decided the introduction to my story needed to start midflight.

I would not be on this plane without my aunt, Lissa. She encouraged me to follow my dream of sharing my sales skills in a most unusual way. Her husband and my uncle, Gary Markwardt, passed away while I was in high school. He had worked for a Fortune 500 company for nearly twenty years.

As he diligently planned his life dreams for post-retirement, he fell ill to a brain tumor that never allowed those dreams to occur. Losing her husband had a profound effect on my aunt. She has since become a life coach and in doing so passionately keeps his memory alive. She has coached numerous people to take chances and achieve their dreams now. Whether it's becoming an elite sales professional or traveling as you write a book, she'll encourage you to do it now.

My destination resulted from my close friend, Steve Weidman. He recommended Cyprus, and I instantly responded that I would go there. Keeping the real reason to myself, I started to tell friends and family that I would be traveling to Cyprus. I then called my aunt to let her know, and she "reminded" me that many years ago my uncle had lived in Nicosia, Cyprus, for three years. As a tribute to my uncle and a thank you to my aunt, I knew Cyprus was the right destination to live and write this book.

I have always had a strong belief that sales are a part of everything we do. No matter what career you choose and no matter where you go, there is always a sales element. These sales lessons are taught to us every day, but whether or not you notice them is up to you. As human beings, we make countless transactions that occur due to some type of psychological impact or inherent need. These decisions can be positive or negative for our health, family, or general well-being.

Throughout my years of coaching sales, it has become my passion to teach sales lessons through unusual stories. In my quest to grow elite sales representatives, I wrote this book as my sales pitch to you. My goal is to sell you on becoming elite.

Most people can relate to traveling, along with the adventures and problems that occur on the way. Sales is a big part of my traveling, whether I want it to be present or not; I just happen to recognize it everywhere I go. I am aware that no matter where I go, I am a salesman. My goal was to narrow in on this portion of my personality and share my story as I adventure and stumble on sales concepts for this book. The result of my travels created an "accidental learning" situation. As you read through my unusual stories, you'll be surprised to find that there is a sales lesson in each one.

I will be systematic in my approach. I will be repetitive. I will excitedly sell you on the concepts in this book at an elite level. However, I will be explicit in how I do so. I have a passion for helping people take their careers to new levels, and at this exact moment, as you read this book, you are my top priority. I'm talking directly to you and gaining your buy-in so that you will embrace these concepts and accelerate your sales career with your current company. You'll learn that it is far easier to grow and care for the green grass beneath you than it is to look for green grass elsewhere—you never know what's on the other side of your fence.

My first lesson in becoming elite is letting you know that you need to stop looking at your neighbor's grass. I can't help you have a green yard if you are constantly moving to a new lawn or peering over the fence with envy. If you are entertaining other job offers, not completely happy in your career, hate your boss, or don't like your commute, you're going to need to solve those problems first.

Everyone needs to be dedicated to their company and their proverbial grass underfoot in order to tackle the challenges of becoming an elite sales representative. It is also vital that you have an honest and ethical product or service, or you could start to cultivate weeds instead of green grass. If you're not completely sure about your situation, you get to make a choice. At any moment you want in life, you can decide to be confident and move full speed ahead in any direction you choose. You get to choose to show up when you want and where you want.

If you want to show up with your current opportunity, you have your yard and it's time to have the greenest grass on the block. You can show up each day to water your grass and accelerate your career. Or you can partake in the cultural epidemic of continually looking for something better every moment of every day.

I'm here to tell you the grass is browner on the other side. My goal is for everyone who reads this book to make strides in their careers by choosing to do so every day with their current company. Your consistent hard work and dedication required each day will be the hardest part of joining the elite. But it's also the best news that I could ever give you. If you want to show up to become an elite sales representative, you can. This book will make sure you have the tools to do so.

Being elite comes with great reward, but it always requires work and effort. Watering and fertilizing your own lawn will provide you with more than just monetary reward. You will be proud to have grown the greenest grass on the block.

As an elite sales professional, you will represent the top two percent of your sales organization. Your colleagues will look to you as the standard for setting the best practices. Your company executives will seek your insight and call upon you to affect change throughout the organization.

Becoming elite is not about getting really good at one aspect of sales. Many successful sales individuals have done so one-dimensionally. You can be successful by mastering the art of networking. You can even be successful by being disciplined and proficient at telemarketing. But to be elite is a process of having a systematic and calculated approach for everything you do. Everyone is given the same amount of hours in a day. The difference is what you do with them.

Throughout this book, you'll be given specific word tracks and power statements that you can use effectively and immediately to help you grow in your career. They will be fill-in-the-blank exercises, so you can input your industry, company, value proposition, and even your own name. Please do so and start using the word tracks and power statements right away. They only work if you use them. Use them with confidence and start selling more today.

For those interested in adding your own personal touch to the word tracks, I encourage you to do so. Your creative and innovative nature will feed and expedite your growth. My word tracks work, but your word tracks will work too. Understanding the concepts is more important than memorizing the exact statements. It's crucial that you sound like yourself and come across as genuine. The ideas and the concepts are what will effectively increase your sales.

As for me, I don't want my new office to be on an airplane. Why does this girl keep looking at my computer screen? Yes, I'm talking to you, seat 30E. Go back to sleep.

1

The Magic Sales Potion

Everyone's story starts somewhere. Your professional story in becoming elite starts with your current position. With 100 percent certainty, I believe the grass is browner everywhere else. I believe my grass is green at this exact moment, and I am excited to water it each day to make it the greenest grass on the block. It's important for you to believe your grass is green like you believe the sky is blue. If it's currently brown, you need to believe that you can water it to make it grow.

We live in a society that is constantly teaching us that the grass is greener on the other side of the proverbial fence. Commercials are fed to us that we need a new car, a better body, a bigger house, or a hotter girlfriend or boyfriend. The list goes on. Everywhere you turn, there is a hyped upgrade that is always needed. We are in such constant search of some magic potion—a material possession that will change an aspect of our lives to "fix" us and make us happy—that we in essence never actually "fix" ourselves.

Show Up

We start our adventure with recognizing the need to actually show up, because truly reading and implementing the concepts in this book will be a lot of work. Showing up is a relative term. Most people never really show up. Most people show up, but they are mentally somewhere else.

Look at the couple who is out to dinner and playing on their phones. They sit across from each other, but they are somewhere else. Look at the student in your class who shows up to sleep. A bed is a better place to take a nap. Look at the countless individuals who show up for work to simply collect a paycheck and leave at 4:59 p.m. so they can go out to dinner and play on their phones.

To show up and become elite in sales is not easy nor is it accidental. There is no magic potion to become elite in sales. If there were, I would bottle it. *Drink your Sales Lemonade once a day and all the sales will come your way.* I'd do commercials, sing jingles, and open up Sales Lemonade stands around the world. But thankfully, I do not have this product because I'm a terrible singer, not to mention the definition of elite would be ruined if all you had to do was drink a magic potion. Elite would become the new normal.

Yes, you are going to have to work for the success you are looking for. And, yes, the grass is browner on the other side as your career upgrade will take much longer if you switch companies. Your grass is immediately brown when you go to a new yard. You'll need to redo a lot of the yardwork that you already did at your current company. Any time you start a position at a new company, you don't even know where the bathroom is, no less how to knock sales records out of the park.

The most important lesson to learn when starting to cultivate your green grass is that you have to show up. It can't be taught, because it is always up to you as to whether or not you "actually" show up. Stop looking at your phone or wondering what else is going on outside of your life, your relationships, and your career. The most important thing for you to do is be present in this exact moment.

This moment is all you really have. If you are waiting for something to happen in the future, it's not here yet. If you are living in the past, it is just a memory and already gone. If you are looking for a moment somewhere else on your phone or computer, you need to realize that you aren't there. You have a choice to go there or show up here, right now.

Showing up and being present in the exact moment is a process I have worked at every day in my career, and it is how I learned elite practices along the way. If I wasn't showing up then, I wouldn't be showing up now. Showing up is the reason I was the Rookie of the Year for a Fortune 1000 company for both units and revenue. I became one of the youngest sales managers at this company and went on to cultivate sales growth with numerous individuals in the sales organization. As a result, I was hired for a new opportunity to build out a sales organization for a start-up based in San Francisco.

Throughout my career, I've taught and coached these elite sales concepts—concepts that seem obvious to most elite sales representatives. Yet many of the concepts I teach go unpracticed by the overwhelming majority of people in sales.

Being elite means doing one thousand and one things on purpose, which includes reading this book. So for everyone who has ever told you that half of life is showing up, I personally thank them for accelerating you on your path to success. Although this book is not meant to explain one thousand and one different sales concepts, this book will help expand your foundation and understanding of how you can show up and take your day-to-day activities to a new level.

Credibility

If you are switching companies or are new to your current company, you have some initial lawn maintenance that you'll need to take care of. It will typically take you a minimum of three months to get up-to-speed on the company. You'll need to learn company information, background, and policies as well as develop internal and external partners as you reset your entire sales process. On day one at your new company, you will learn where the bathroom is and some of the names of your peers. You will have zero prospects that you have presented your new product to. Not only does this mean you have not perfected your presentation, but it means your pipeline is next to nothing.

Some sales representatives may argue that if you stay in the same industry, you will not be starting from ground zero to rebuild your pipeline. However, your initial yardwork will now require that you reestablish the credibility of your new company and yourself. It will require time to re-secure relationships that had grown to trust you and the credibility of your previous company.

In many instances, you may lose external networking partners as a result of your transition. The most important way to minimize your losses will be your selection of an honest and ethical company with a product or service that you can trust. Likewise, your networking partners may understand your transition as they continue to support and work with you.

Credibility is essential in your path to becoming an elite sales representative. In fact, it's essential in anything you do. Not many people want a surgeon to operate on them right out of medical school. Credibility is important in every industry and especially in sales to provide your prospect and referral sources with the confidence that they can trust you.

I'd reached the Moscow airport and was still half asleep when I had my own credibility challenged. I was standing in line for a coffee during my layover, and I met Alice, who was traveling with her husband, Jack. I heard her speaking English as her husband came over and requested she order him a pastry while we were in line. The line was long, so I introduced myself as I was curious where they were from. They were from Wales, and they were on holiday. She was curious what I was doing in Russia from California as she inquired about my travels.

As we discussed my travels and my journey to write this book on sales, I realized that my current credibility as an author was not where I wanted it to be after one simple question from Alice. "How many books have you published?" Because this book would be my first, I responded honestly at the time that I hadn't published any. I perceived that this book would be the first of multiple sales and leadership books that I would write, but I could tell she immediately questioned my validity as an author.

As I continued to stand in line to get my coffee, it became clear that, as someone new to the literary world, I was standing on brown grass. While I was excited about this new opportunity in my career, my lawn would need some serious work. So I set out with the determination to show up each day and water it moving forward.

Establishing credibility in a new position takes time. As my tenure grew, my response and credibility grew with it. I would later formulate a different response to this question on my travels with renewed confidence.

Tenure

Tenure is the number-one commonality of all elite sales representatives. Interview the top sales representative of a hundred different, *established* companies, and over 80 percent will have tenure of two-plus years. No one can force you to stay at your current position. In fact, you'll have recruiters, friends, and family members all tell you that you are underpaid and too talented for your current position. They will encourage you that the grass is greener on the other side, and they will ineffectively set you back in your career if they are able to "sell" you on it.

I have worked for multiple sales organizations, and I can tell you that the biggest struggle across the board for creating elite teams is turnover. Sales organizations demand a lot from their employees. Just to learn the product or service, you will need to run fast in one direction. But you'll also need to run in a multitude of other directions at the same time to build your network and prospects and create immediate impact with your sales at your new company. The learning curve, rejection, and overall workload is intimidating and frustrating to many of the representatives who come on board.

While sales provides an opportunity to control your own income by selling more, many representatives leave prior to establishing themselves in their new career. If they only knew their grass was green, I believe many more would stick around to watch it grow.

When someone leaves within their first year, leadership cannot effect success or failure. It is impossible to help someone achieve success when they do not provide the company with the one thing the company and the sales representative needs. Tenure. Tenure is an absolute necessity in becoming elite. No matter how hard your new position is, your grass will get greener when you stick it out and water it every day.

I encourage everyone on my team to discuss the process with their friends and family. Let your support system know you've made a career decision that you need their support on.

Tell them the first six months of your new position will be demanding as you transition your career. However, if you work hard the first six months, the dividends will vastly pay off for the future of your career and your workload will not always be like this.

I believe that all opportunities worth taking are worth investing a minimum of one year. When someone is with a company for less than one year, the question I concentrate on in an interview is this: "What went wrong?"

For the importance of your resume and future career opportunities, you should never willingly leave a company prior to one year of tenure. It is not only vital for building your credibility in your quest to become elite, it is also vital in building the credibility of your resume. Being at a company for less than one year is a failure on multiple levels for all involved.

As we move on to chapter 2 of this book, I will reiterate that you must establish your current position as home before striving to become elite. Continually looking at the bigger house and proverbially bigger yard will never allow you to water your own grass. As I conclude this chapter, please fill in the following sentence with your company's name. This will be your first power statement. Power statements are statements that you must believe in order to take steps forward in your pursuit of becoming elite.

My home is at _____.
(Your Company)

2

A Bed For My Backpack

I spent a night in the Moscow airport on my way to Cyprus. How I found a flight with a twenty-hour layover and still purchased it is currently beyond me. I may not have been on a timetable, but who wants to spend twenty hours in an airport? I learn sales lessons from everyone though, and I'm constantly evaluating anyone I meet who provides me with a sales pitch. I had a great one as I rented a capsule hotel from Marina.

Marina was from Russia, and it was very clear her English was not fluent. But she is one of the most confident people I have ever met. While I continued to make her repeat what she was saying, she looked at me as if I were a moron for not understanding her poor English. Better yet, she was selling me on what a great deal it was for me to be renting a room with two beds.

Keep in mind, I'm not traveling with anyone, and this is a hotel in an airport that rents rooms by the hour for overnight travelers to catch a little rest in between their flights. Having a second bed for an additional cost wouldn't do me any good. But since she was out of single bedrooms, she was attempting to convince me this was a fantastic deal that I needed to hop on right away.

I didn't know there were no single bedrooms. I was completely confused; I thought that it must be a shared room. I really couldn't tell if her English was poor or if I needed to hire her for a sales position. I explained that I wanted a private room, and through much more dialogue it became clear to me that it was in fact a private room; she just didn't have any single bedrooms available.

I had finally processed the situation with my foggy and tired brain. I'd stumbled on the best sales representative in all of Russia. She was fumbling through her poor English and selling me on the larger room because it's all she had. I'm not used to having someone more confident than I am in a sales situation, but I was having trouble understanding her and was low on sleep. Regardless, I had to take control of the conversation.

"Do you have any rooms with three beds?" I said as I stood by myself. Marina and the male Russian sitting next to her behind the desk stared back at me blankly as my question made no sense due to our previous conversation and my request for a single bed. There was no laughter to be found. I'm barely funny to someone who speaks fluent English, and my joke wasn't very good. But I was curious if she would try to sell me on three beds and what the price was.

After what seemed like a long pause, she responded, "No, I only have rooms with two beds open. You need to book now before someone else comes; we don't have many rooms left." And with the hard close, I was wide awake.

I needed to investigate her sales pitch a little more. I was no longer the best salesperson in the room, so I had to make her work for it. I decided to see how she pitched me on six hours of rental time versus seven.

"Seven is better." No real explanation as to why, but "seven is better." As I had her break down the cost, it didn't really seem like seven was a better deal at all. At the same time, she said it with so much confidence that it made sense to me.

I wanted to get some sleep, and the extra hour would be worth whatever the cost was going to be—I had no idea how rubles exchanged for dollars. With all the appreciation in the world for a great sales presentation, I booked my two beds for seven hours. My backpack and I each had our own bed to sleep in. If half the job of being an elite sales representative is showing up, the other half of the job has everything to do with confidence.

The First A: Accountability

I believe there are four As to being successful in sales, and accountability is the first. Holding yourself accountable is more about confidence than anything else. Marina's confidence in her two-bedroom, seven-hour room had me completely sold. In retrospect, I wasn't in an exasperating rush to get my room. The reality was it would have cost substantially less to go have a beer at the bar and come back when the single bedroom was available later in the evening.

There is nothing more important than the ability to say, "I am." Marina showed up and said, "I am an English-speaking, elite salesperson." When I questioned her, she looked at me as though I'd tried to tell her the sky wasn't blue.

I've spent most of my life holding myself accountable by simply stating "I am." I ran division-two track at my first college in South Dakota, but I transferred to the University of San Diego my junior year. While my experience water-skiing was not at a level where I should have been on a team competing in the NCWSA (National Collegiate Water Ski Association), by telling myself, "I am a water-skier," I eventually told myself, "I am the captain of the USD water-ski team." And further, "I am the coach of the USD water-ski team."

I immediately took my "I am" concept to the business world where I proudly exclaimed that I am the rookie of the year. Please don't misinterpret these statements. Holding yourself accountable should not be standing on a table and telling everyone else you are better than they are. In fact, it's quite the opposite. Holding yourself accountable is telling a select group of people who already believe in you and will follow up with you on your statement.

Your "I am" statement should be told to your closest friends, family members, and a small and select group of peers that you work with. Telling someone that you barely know comes across as cocky, as if you're tooting your own horn. Telling someone you are close to is sharing something intimate and personal. They should understand this and feel excited to follow up with you on your goal and progress.

The biggest part of your "I am" statement is asking these close friends and family members to hold you accountable. You need to ask people in your life who will be excited to follow up with you, understand your passion and excitement of your goal, and believe that you will achieve it. Everyone outside of your support network can think as they please.

Please take a moment to take your first step in becoming elite. But make sure that you make it your own. Write down your "I am" power statement. It will be one of the most important power statements in the entire book.

Here are some examples: *I am in the top 2 percent of my sales organization. I am the number-one sales representative of my entire company. I am the rookie of the year.*

Say it over and over again. Once you believe it the same way that you believe the sky is blue, you are ready to share it. Be careful about whom you share it with. You are looking for people who believe in you, will follow up with you, hold you accountable to what you've told them, and who will be supportive if you start to doubt your statement.

I am .

For the past two years, I have told multiple people that I am going to write a book. The first time I told someone was almost ten years prior to typing my first word on the flight to Moscow. I started by telling my sales mentor, Tom Riley, and the process began. I eventually told my parents. And over the past two years, as I found that I needed more accountability to take the next steps, I told approximately forty people that I consider supporters of my continued professional growth and development. As a result, I'm excited to show up for chapter 2 with this statement: "I am an author."

The second part to holding yourself accountable is dressing the part. Dressing the part should be in every aspect of your life to truly embrace your "I am" statement. The number-one sales representative in the entire company doesn't wear worn-out shoes and a loose tie. I'm not asking that you take out a loan and buy an Armani suit. However, it will be hard for you to believe your own "I am" statement if you aren't dressing professionally. Believe in yourself and physically change how you look in the mirror as you dress the part.

There are plenty of places to find discounted, professional dress. If you are in outside sales and your company doesn't require professional dress, dress better than every other sales representative in the office. Your "I am" statement requires professional dress even though your company does not. Prospects don't want to buy from someone in a polo or, worse, a T-shirt. Companies want to buy from someone who looks professional and who they feel is trustworthy.

You will learn to enjoy dressing the part. I was well known at my first sales position for wearing a fitted suit every single day. There were times that the office went casual, and I still dressed like the boss. Dressing as a professional sends a message. It lets everyone know you are serious about your job and that you intend to do it like a professional. Whether your current role is inside sales or outside sales, dressing the part sends a message to yourself and everyone else in the company. You will believe your "I am" statement more in a fitted suit than you will in a T-shirt.

The Second A: Activity

The second A is a direct result of the first. When you hold yourself accountable, you will increase your activity. In sports, each athlete that embraces their coach holding them accountable finds new levels of activity once thought impossible. It's absolutely no different in the world of sales. You won't be elite if you don't work harder than the other representatives, and the best way to do so is to have your coach (ideally, your manager) and the closest people in your life holding you accountable. As a direct result of these people holding you accountable, your activity always goes up.

> **Caution: Make sure you believe your "I am" statement before you start telling your boss, your closest friends, and family members. You may not want people holding you accountable for something that you don't really believe in or maybe don't want to do.**

Not everyone is in a position to grow into an elite sales professional. You may have things in your life that will hold you back, and that's okay. Life is often a balance between what we want to do and what we have to do. But this book was not written for those who are being held back. This book was written for those that are willing to concentrate on becoming elite without allowing excuses to dictate their success.

The best news I can give you is that it is much harder to become elite than maintain it. The investment you make in yourself, your career, and your sales skills now will pay dividends for the rest of your life. This is why it is important that your closest friends and family are holding you accountable as much as you are. No one becomes elite on their own. Their support will be intricate to your success. Make sure you have it before you proceed with your "I am" statement.

Once it's out there, you will have to work for your results. But the good news is your results will come; they have to. As I continued to tell more people that I am an author, I watched an interesting effect occur. I begin to email myself with ideas for this book like a crazy person. I found that I enjoyed sending emails to myself. My subject line was *book*, and I would move all of these emails into a folder that would eventually formulate the outline of what you are reading today. The accountability that I had given myself increased my activity to a point where I went from someone who wanted to write a book to someone who knew his chapters, the style, the title, and a bulk of what he wanted to say.

Over the years, I've watched many representatives achieve phenomenal performances by simply stating "I am." I once managed a representative who was outlandishly behind his goal of winning a trip to the company's conference event. It was his first year selling, and accomplishing this achievement was a big deal. However, the chips were stacked against him going into the last month. Although this was true, he'd made up his mind that he'd already achieved the goal. As we got closer to the end of the year, I only told him one thing, "You are a conference rep. I'm not sure how you'll get there, but I know you will." I would then repeat, "You are a conference rep."

The more you and the people around you say your "I am" statement, the more it becomes real. It became so engrained in his mind that he was a "conference rep", he achieved what many thought he should not have been able to achieve. At over 300 percent of his quota for the month, he achieved what was merely a formality.

He out-sold every single sales representative in Southern California on total units for the month, including the representative who was the number-one salesperson for the entire company that year. While the rest of Southern California had no idea how this new representative produced at such an elite level, I can confidently say someone would have had an easier time convincing him that the sky wasn't blue over convincing him that he wasn't a "conference rep."

Once you become elite, it is much easier to maintain it because the mind and the body understand what needs to be done in order to achieve the goal. The following fiscal year, this same representative was striving for a much higher goal. As we headed into the last month of the fiscal, with an even loftier month needed than the previous year, we simply discussed the exact same process and agreed that he was already there. It was then just a matter of doing the work. He did the work and once again achieved his lofty goal of success.

The Third A: Attitude

The first and second A do not matter if you don't have the right *attitude*. As you've probably read in countless sales and leadership books, your attitude will dictate your success. While you may not always feel like it, you have complete control of your attitude.

Quite often in life, we find exactly what we're looking for. Attitude and belief help shape and mold our lives. Believe that your life is terrible, and everything goes wrong. You will continue to uncover more problems while you are looking in the wrong direction. If you choose to see that life is a gift, you will uncover the joy of each and every situation you encounter. While our emotions are wired to tell us a particular story based on sadness or anger, our brains can choose to tell our emotions what is perfect about our feelings and how we can learn, grow and enjoy each situation.

Never have I had a person demonstrate everything that's right and wrong with attitude at the same time than a young woman who worked for me named Jamie. When Jamie was working in her small bubble of sales, there was no one who worked harder and put in a better day than she did. However, when something went wrong in her day, Jamie would completely derail. The unfortunate reality is she wouldn't just derail *her* day. She would derail anyone and everyone who was willing to listen to her stories and complaints. Stopping your day to listen to office gossip will consistently produce less activity for you and the other person. Not only does your attitude affect your production, but it affects the production of those around you.

As important as it is to control your own attitude, it is equally important to control the time you spend with those around you. I believe that you should treat anyone with a negative attitude as if they have the plague. Steer clear of any "Jamies" you meet at all costs. They will waste your day by complaining about their problems, and the plague is catchy.

No matter how hard you try, you will eventually catch their bad attitude. It is extremely important you surround yourself with successful people who encourage you to your own success and do not complain. Negative attitudes in one way or another eventually lead to poor business practices and in some cases even unethical practices. No sales leader wants their sales organization to catch the negative plague. Please realize that not only is having a good attitude a requirement of becoming elite, it is often a requirement for maintaining your employment.

The Fourth A: Awesome

I'm human. And so are you. We all have emotions, and it is completely normal to feel sad, mad, upset, or whatever else you're feeling. But it's what you do with those emotions that affect your production. Everyone has a choice to make when something goes wrong. But having a good attitude is just the start. The fourth A is choosing to be awesome.

"Be Awesome."

Your girlfriend or boyfriend can break up with you, and you can decide not to show up. Maybe it's a perfect sick day. Or maybe it's a better day to physically show up but spend the entire day talking to your peers and boss about your terrible breakup.

You always get a choice. While you are working, I ask that you choose to be awesome. If you need the personal time, please take it so that when you come back to work you'll be the awesome person you know you can be. If you choose not to take the personal time, choose to be awesome at work and effectively have your great workday carry into your personal evening. Just as your personal life can transfer into work, let being awesome at work provide an energy boost for your personal life.

Everyone appreciates positivity and an awesome attitude. Seek out the elite professionals in your office and take them to lunch. Awesome will breed awesome. You will find that you can help elevate someone else's success as much as they can elevate your own.

Elite sales professionals will spread awesomeness as though it's contagious. When an elite professional generates excitement from stories of their own success, their peers gravitate to them and these elite practices become replicated throughout the office. Choose to seek out these individuals and feed off of their energy.

An awesome attitude should not be locked up in solitary confinement.

Recapping the Four As

I am back in the air on my flight to Larnaca, Cyprus. Sitting next to me is a Russian male, in his mid-fifties, with his hand on his forehead and half asleep. He was the kind gentleman who asked to take my window seat when I got on the plane. For some reason, he thought I'd be excited to sit in the middle. He's wearing a pink polo that doesn't appear to fit him right, but maybe it's just the color that makes it look like the wrong wardrobe choice. I never understand why any guy thinks he can pull off a pink shirt. He's currently dressing the part of "guy I wish I was not sitting next to." But I'm still showing up as an author with a smile on my face. I am choosing to be awesome.

It's all about making a choice to be positive about the situation. You have to understand that the break up with your manipulative, lying girlfriend has nothing to do with your actual job. In fact, it doesn't prevent you from making that extra call and being more awesome than every other sales representative you're competing against. It should actually encourage you to do so.

When my personal life isn't going the way I want it to, the last thing I want to do is have my life affect the way my career is going. Boris and his pink shirt did not prevent me from busting out chapter two on this flight. So whatever you have going on in your personal life, please ignore it and choose to be awesome. And for those of you who need that extra push, please make sure you are utilizing your friends and family to hold you accountable to kicking butt. *If needed, please ask them to kick yours.*

As we conclude this chapter, please make sure to continue your work on your "I am" statement. You don't get to share it until you believe it like you believe the sky is blue. Memorize the four As to success. They will be instrumental in your becoming elite.

1. Accountability
2. Activity
3. Attitude
4. Awesome

And if the mood strikes you, take a break from reading to do a little shopping. You need to dress the part. See you later Boris; I'm about to land in Cyprus!

3

Crying Creates Obligation

I'm lying on a beach in Limassol and staring out at the Mediterranean Sea. The view is incredible as I look out at the rocks and the multicolored blue sea. I'm finally here! I just want to lie here and do nothing other than work on my tan. It seems like forever since I had no responsibility in the world, and at this exact moment, there is no one who could make me do anything.

I feel shallow writing that all I wanted to do is work on my tan, so I feel the need to clarify. Having a nice tan is not my top priority in life, but I have the worst farmer's tan I've ever had. I was in Minnesota golfing with one of my best friends, Dan Dahl, prior to my trip and developed a Neapolitan skin color on my arms. The farmer's tan is the single greatest downside to golfing. Coming in a close second place is my drive off of nearly every tee box.

My schedule for the afternoon was to lie on my back for fifteen minutes, jump in the sea, lie on my stomach for fifteen minutes and jump in the sea. Repeat over and over until I left this oasis of a beach to go grab some local Cypriot food. Even as I'm relaxing, I have a plan.

I once had an ex-girlfriend tell me that God laughs at us when we make plans. It's a great quote, but I think it was her way of telling me she was sick of my planning. I quickly explained, "Successful people plan and execute every single day." Being elite happens on purpose. It does not happen by accident.

"Successful people plan and execute every single day."

As ridiculous as my plan was for relaxing on the beach, I was about to be laughed at. A woman in non-beach apparel sat down next to my towel about 20 feet away. I looked over as I found it interesting that it was nearly 90 degrees, and she was clearly not dressed for the beach. I just got here and I'm fitting in better than she is. She was wearing large sunglasses, an embroidered and decorative shirt, and jeans. As she tucked her knees into her chest, she began to shake uncontrollably. As she wiped her eyes from beneath her sunglasses, I knew she was not okay.

I know not everyone is going to interrupt their personal schedule for someone they've never met before. But this poor woman was crying as she looked out at one of the most beautiful beaches I'd ever seen. How could I be lying here in complete happiness and relaxation and have her experiencing such a different situation a mere 20 feet away?

I had a million thoughts going through my head as to why she was crying. Maybe her mom just died. Her boyfriend dumped her. She recently quit a high-paying executive position in the United States to become an author and she has writer's block.

Regardless, it's okay to not be okay. And sometimes someone reaching out to let you know they care is all a person needs. I'm happy to help someone in need whenever I am physically able. And I would even take it one step further to explain that I feel obligated to do so when I'm placed in this type of situation.

If I were superman, crying would be my kryptonite. I am, however, not superman, and my current tan has me afraid that my stomach may blind her as the sun reflects off me. But she's wearing sunglasses and due to my curiosity and concern for this woman's general well-being, I felt obligated to approach her.

Be Curious

My curiosity was a part of why I was going to walk over to this woman crying on the beach. And interestingly enough, one of the consistent traits I've found with elite sales representatives is that they are inherently curious.

The reason why being curious is a part of those who are elite is because they are able to ask the uncomfortable questions to get to the bottom of the reason why someone is hesitating to buy or refer. They do the best needs analysis. And they connect better with the prospect because they get to know their business, their desires, and the reasons why they are even there with the opportunity to sell.

If you are not innately curious, I have great news for you. Curiosity can be learned. Allow any five-year-old to teach you, as we take a lesson from the girl I call Princess 3. (Her older sisters are Princess 1 and Princess 2.) Here was our interaction some months ago:

"Why aren't you married?" Regan asked me while we were playing.

"Well, because I haven't found the right person yet."

"Why?" Regan responds again.

I respond with more information knowing that it will probably not be sufficient. "Well, because the girls I've dated haven't been right for me."

"Why?" Regan responds even more enthusiastically.

"They just haven't been the right girls for me to marry and spend the rest of my life with. They aren't nice enough. I want to marry someone really nice."

"Why?" Regan responds yet again as I start to feel exasperated.

"Well, Regan. If I don't marry someone nice, they may not let me play with you and that wouldn't be fun. You want me to be able to play with you, right?" I said this with the hope that I'd derailed her "why" questions with a question of my own.

"Yes, let's go play monkey in the middle." I already knew who the monkey was, but I was just happy to stop the "why" campaign on this subject.

The valuable lesson any five-year-old can teach you is that we learn the most on second-, third-, and fourth-level questions. Elite sales representatives aren't afraid to ask why or go more in-depth. We will find out exactly what we need to know. While my answer to Regan may have skipped over some of the details as to why I'm single, it's a great demonstration on how second- and third-level questions can extract additional information.

"Be Curious."

I stood up to walk over to the crying woman on the beach with the minimum knowledge of what to say right away. When I'm abroad, I only have one opening line. I'm hesitant that people may not understand me, so I open with, "Do you speak English?" She responded that she did, so I went with my second line. "Hi, I'm Jon."

"Hello. I'm Dilyana."

I smiled with a certain amount of hesitation. "I just wanted to see if you were okay." As I listened to her response, I sat down next to her and peered out at the sea, enjoying my view. We went on to talk for ten minutes.

Dilyana had just moved to Cyprus for the summer from Bulgaria to be with her mom, who lived here. She was working at a restaurant all day long and had just left the restaurant to sit on the beach and cry. She was lonely and missed her friends and home back in Bulgaria. I was happy and feeling the freedom of the warm sun and the blue sea. She was sad and feeling the prison of a summer away from her friends and the town she grew up in.

We talked for a while and, to some extent, I hope that I made her feel better. She was young and unsure about life, but she was confident that she wasn't happy here. I went back to my beach towel and jumped back in the sea. As I exited the sea, she motioned for me to come back over. She wanted my phone number, so we could hang out.

Looks like my pep talk worked, but in the wrong direction. With full intentions to enjoy this time on my own and write, I can sincerely say that I wasn't interested. I smiled and took her number. I intended to text her at least once as I felt obligated, yet again. I wouldn't want her to feel more sad and blown off.

As I type this, I pause and send a quick text message to Dilyana: "Hey Dilyana. It's Jon from the beach. I'm just writing my book and wanted to say hi and have an awesome day!" With that, I felt as though I'd fulfilled my obligations and hoped that Dilyana found happiness over the rest of her summer in Cyprus.

Perception is reality. Let me repeat this statement how I view it, because it is important. Your perception is your reality. If you perceive that you are in the most beautiful spot in the world and couldn't be happier, you are indeed, at that moment, happy. And if you perceive that you are trapped on a terrible island and would rather be anywhere else, you are indeed, in that moment, sad. It's time to remember the third A is by far the most powerful one, because your attitude can cause you to go to an amazing beach and cry rather than feel awesome.

For the past five years, I've been telling those I'm holding myself accountable to that there will be an entire chapter on obligation. So it's only appropriate that after learning the four As, our mission to become elite starts here. Professional obligation is the best way to effectively increase your closing ratio.

Let's take another lesson from a different princess as we turn to Princess 1. If Krimzen wants to play with one of her sister's toys, the fastest way to create obligation is by saying, "Mom, Brooklyn isn't sharing." Krimzen's sales pitch goes directly to a point of influence that elevates the likelihood that she will close her sale. While no one closes at 100 percent, Krimzen closes at a very high ratio.

In this scenario, Princess 2 will often have to relinquish her toy and share. While I love my goddaughter, Brooklyn, I'm consistently impressed with a great sales pitch. Awesome job, Princess 1!

Being elite, means you cannot be above screaming, "Mom!" If something can effectively bring me to a higher closing ratio, I will use professional obligation to increase the likelihood that I will get my sale. In the world of professional sales, "Mom" comes in many forms and varieties.

Obligation is in all sales. At a certain point, your prospect is committed to moving forward. And to a certain extent, they will feel bad if they don't. You or an outside influence has created this obligatory situation. Learning how to create professional obligation for moving forward will be key to your success.

Be Persistent

I spent the majority of my days in Limassol writing at the Yellow Lounge Café on the promenade right by the sea. As we talk about professional obligation, I can tell you there is no greater formulation of professional obligation than professional persistence. Ironically, I've already recognized that persistence will be the largest driver in the successful completion of this book.

Persistence should never mean being annoying or pushy. In elite sales, it means providing professional and courteous follow-up. In order to do so, all professional sales require some type of customer relationship management, or CRM, tool. You need a way to document your notes and follow up. Without it, you are following up like every other sales representative or, even worse, missing follow-up calls that will cost you sales and money. In order to be elite, you need to be a detective.

Like any great detective, you are building a case. Your case is to prove beyond a reasonable doubt that buying from you is the right thing to do for the prospect and their business. In order to do this, it is important you document your notes along the way as you professionally follow up. Here's a great example of a word track for someone following up as a professional.

"Hey, Matt. How have you been? That's great.

I was just thinking of you the other day when the Vikings beat the Packers. Congratulations on the big win. (Discuss)

The reason for my call is I wanted to follow up from our meeting two weeks ago to discuss moving forward with _____. Last time we
(Your Company)
talked about _____
(Value Proposition 1)
and _____ being beneficial
(Value Proposition 2)
to your business. I'm going to be in your area on Thursday afternoon and would like to continue our discussion and further discuss _____
(New Value Point)
as I know it will benefit your business. Are you available Thursday at three?"

As you can see from the sample word track, your CRM tool needs to be used to document personal information about your prospect and professional information, and it should be time stamped. A CRM tool creates obligation. Whether you are commenting on where their daughter is going to school, their favorite football team, or what you've discussed previously, you are proving your credibility and your right to earn their business.

A CRM tool is effectively a note to yourself on how you should communicate to your prospect at a time in the future that is set strategically. You will need to learn appropriate timelines for follow-up specific to your business and your company through trial and error. You should always err on the side of following up too soon with a quick apology as opposed to waiting too long and missing out on your sale.

No one has ever had more professional obligation to sign up for a company from my CRM than Jacob of Fresh Floral in San Diego. Jacob was one of my first sales presentations in my selling career. I met with him for a formal sales presentation every six months with consistent follow-up in between and random visits when I was in the area.

On my call to line up our fourth appointment, I said, "Jacob, I met with you almost two years ago, and we discussed how my company would benefit you. I trained you on our product and discussed the differences between us and your current provider. Since our first meeting, we've met two more times where we've discussed the features and why I believe this is the best solution for your company. I'm calling to find out if you can meet with me on Thursday at three and find out what it's going to take to win your business."

It was a mouthful and there was no immediate response on the other end. Jacob started to chuckle a little, knowing that he'd never get rid of me until he signed up. "Jon, you're still with that company?" It was his most honest and sincere response that he could give.

I started laughing myself. "Yes, it's a great company. That's why I know it's the right decision for your business."

Jacob laughed. "Okay, Jon. You got me. Just give me a good discount on the pricing and I'll come on board."

Jacob felt obligated to come on board by the work I'd done to gain his business. But if he wanted a discount, he'd need to feel a different level of professional obligation. I'm good at what I do and don't like working for a discounted commission.

When we met, I let him know that I'd be willing to give him a discount, but he'd have to earn it. He needed to personally introduce me to another business owner he knew and endorse

Crying Creates Obligation

me. I was also very clear that he couldn't tell them the discount that I offered him. Jacob laughed again as I could tell he was impressed with my professionalism, persistence, and sales skills. He let me know that he'd worked in sales before owning this business and that he'd do me one better. He said, "Come with me."

With that, Jacob pulled down the garage-type door of his flower shop, and we walked next door to a coffee shop. "Mary, this is Jon. He helps my company and is a great guy. You need to sign up with him. Can you meet with him after I'm done talking to him?"

Mary responded that tomorrow after the morning rush would be better. She asked that I come by at two.

I was impressed. She didn't even know what I did or what company I was with. But Jacob did a masterful job of selling me and my importance to his company. Jacob had most definitely been in sales before. He'd created professional obligation for Mary to sign up, and everything pushed forward when we met. I signed up Mary the next day with no discount.

I've already given you a lot of great news on how to become elite. But my personal favorite is that being elite is a compounding equation when you do it correctly. It will allow you to gain sales en masse instead of one at a time. Jacob is a small example of professional obligation creating more than one sale in one instant. But when you think in mass quantities, you can start to see how consistently practicing elite activities will generate sales from multiple and completely different avenues at any time on any given day.

Professional follow-up is not limited to a well-crafted phone call. Some of my best follow-ups resulted when other sales representatives were watching TV. I love sending articles to people I'm prospecting or networking with. In my opinion, there is no better time to send that article than at night or on the weekend. With the advancement of technology and the smartphone, it can literally take under ten seconds to send an article to a prospect.

For example, here's an email: "Hey, Matt. I saw the Vikings beat the Packers, and I was just reading this article that I thought you'd enjoy. Go Vikings! –Jon"

Professional sales is all about creating inbound calls. Matt will be responding to my email or calling me in the near future after I sent him the Vikings article. He'll be further impressed and obligated to respond if he knows I took time out of my personal schedule to send him that article.

While an article on the Vikings may be fun for Matt, sending an email on a business tax law change or something in their industry is even better. Be seen as a consultant and someone their business needs. Even better, articles on tax law changes and industry articles can be copied and pasted in emails to multiple prospects. All you'll need to do is change the name of who you're sending it to and the first couple of lines to personalize it. And make sure you do.

There is more obligation to a personalized email than there is to a mass email. Depending on your company's investment in technology, you may even have the ability for customization of these emails without typing each person's name. Investing in the right technology will help with your efficiency and ability to tackle the one thousand and one tasks necessary to become elite.

Be Persuasive

There is absolutely nothing wrong with being persuasive. Come on. You're in sales! If you don't want to be persuasive, pick a different career. I enjoy selling. And I enjoy convincing you that I am the best solution for your company. The primary reason someone buys is you. Not the company. Jacob bought because he believed in me and my professional follow-up. He knew that if he signed up with me, I would be there to help him and his business.

Being persuasive means you'll ask for the business and obligate your prospect to move forward. But professional persuasion always answers the why question. There is nothing more important to becoming elite than being able to close. But you need to learn to close the correct way.

As you close your prospects, you need to make sure they understand why it's such a great deal to be signing up with you. Use the words, "You're getting a great deal." Those words should immediately be followed with the why. This is where you reiterate the value points of your company. And it is important you do. You are at the most crucial portion of the sales process, and you need to make sure your prospects understand the value they are getting for their money.

Almost every sales book will teach you the importance of ABC—always be closing. Ironically, it is a sales concept that I completely disagree with even though we could spend the next eighty pages on the concept of closing businesses from an elite standpoint.

ABS, Not ABC

I believe in ABS. ABS is not what you get from five hundred sit-ups every morning. ABS stands for always be selling. ABS is a concept that I have lived by since I started selling over ten years ago. If you are in sales, it should be obvious that when the situation is presented you need to close to earn their business. As a result, I try to coach the less obvious.

ABS—always be selling

Elite sales representatives are always selling and, as a result, create a different type of obligation as they do so. Make sure you have your business cards in your wallet or purse. Make sure during all your personal conversations that you discuss what you do and ask your friends and family members for business and referrals. And realize that every situation is a sales call.

I've never had a sales representative better embrace ABS as Katie did for me when I first taught her the concept. Katie took public transportation every day into work. And the next morning after she learned ABS, she stopped playing with her phone on her morning commute. She decided to strike up a conversation with the person next to her, who happened to be a business owner. ABS meant she should always be selling, and why shouldn't she be selling on her ride into work? The lady sitting next to her provided her with three referrals and committed to sign up her own business with Katie.

This happened because Katie created professional obligation while she sat next to the woman on the bus. By befriending her neighbor, she was not a pushy salesperson trying to get her business. She was a friendly stranger explaining what she did for a living. The lady she had met had no idea that Katie was on a sales call. After all, the lady was just talking to a nice stranger during her own commute. Katie showed up that morning, and she was awesome.

Winning breeds winning, and losing breeds losing. If your attitude embraces these concepts and practices them, they will work. Surround yourself with others who embrace these same concepts; they will infectiously become a part of how you operate on a day-to-day basis.

No concept works 100 percent of the time. But these concepts are proven and work for elite sales representatives. In order for you to also believe in them and use them in everyday practice, you must utilize them until you achieve success. Once you do, it's impossible for someone to convince you not to do them. I am happy to share that Katie still uses ABS and that was not the only sale that Katie got from her commute.

HELP

It is the greatest four-letter word to generate professional obligation. It can be used in multiple avenues but will only work effectively with straightforward sincerity. And if you don't use it, it never works.

From a psychological standpoint, humans innately want to help other humans. Whether you feel that urge to hold a door open for someone, help pick up papers that were dropped, or even stop to help someone with a flat tire on the side of the road, we are designed as such for our own benefit as much as for the other person. It truly is people helping people.

Please help me demonstrate this concept by making it your mission to do one act of kindness prior to the end of the day. You will find there is inherent joy associated with it and why one of my favorite words in sales is *help*.

There is also growing scientific evidence from many studies as to why humans innately want to help other humans. Regardless of whether you are what the general public would consider a "nice person" or not, there are studies being done on what is known as the "helper's high." These studies believe helping someone can reduce one's own stress.

Studies have demonstrated longer lifespans and less disease in those who habitually volunteer in some shape or form. One large study for older adults found a 44 percent reduction in early death among those who volunteered a lot. This showed a greater effect than exercising four times a week.

While these studies are relatively new to the end of the twentieth century, it is important to note the psychological presence of this particular sales concept. I truly believe that understanding psychology is part of becoming a member of the professional elite, so understanding the helper's high may not only help you de-stress but help you sell more.

As you use the word *help* to effectively generate more referrals and sales, you will need to use it more than once. Be repetitive and, remember, your prospects and referral sources innately want to help you. Do them a favor and allow them to de-stress by giving you a referral as you ask for their help.

As I write this, I feel like an absolute hypocrite. I've spent my entire day at a restaurant. I had a coffee in the morning, followed by a late lunch, and I'm about to order a beer and follow it up with a late dinner. There did not appear to be anywhere to plug in my laptop other than a location where I can't sit. As my computer died twice, I plugged it in and recharged the battery.

I'm embarrassed to say that for the last seven hours I've been here, I never once asked for help. Asking for help would have given me a much different result. I know this because the wait staff just changed and Mario saw me moving my computer to the corner of the room where he knew I couldn't use it. He immediately shook his head no and said that he would help me. He literally said, "Let me help you." I feel embarrassed writing this, but being an elite salesman does not mean being perfect. Everyone makes mistakes.

Mario switched my table to the other side of the restaurant, and I am now plugged in and typing. The real embarrassment is that when I had my computer plugged in and charging in the corner, I was no longer "showing up" for my day. I was playing on my phone in a completely unproductive way with some game that I had downloaded. I wasn't enjoying the beach or doing anything productive. I was in Cyprus, but my mind was elsewhere.

It's easy to not show up. But being elite also means we recognize our mistakes and get better. I let the language barrier be an excuse for not showing up and asking for help. I refuse to do this again on the rest of my trip.

Help in a professional setting is different, but it actually works the same way and creates great professional obligation. Let's go through a few scenarios with word tracks. Use the word tracks in each different scenario to see how the professional obligation you've created allows you to sell more.

On a sales call where you don't get the business, say this:

> Stand up as though you are going to walk away and say, "I really appreciate your time and am sorry we aren't a better fit for your company. Just to help me with my future presentations, do you mind telling me what my company could do differently that would have won your business today?"

This is my favorite "walk away close." Most of the time, they will tell you exactly what you need to know. In a best-case scenario, you will be able to sit back down and apologize that you didn't cover their response during your presentation and still win the business. In a worst-case scenario, you can use the second-level help question and get a referral:

> "No problem. I completely understand and appreciate your help. While I may not be a good fit for your business, I can tell you probably know a lot of other companies. Do you know anyone that you can refer me to in order to discuss _____? I would really appreciate
> (Your Company)
> it, and it would really help me out."

If you are in inside sales, both of these word tracks still work, but you would just say, "Before I let you go," after your presentation. Also, get specific on the referral. It often leads to a greater likelihood they refer you.

On a sales call that is going to require a discount to win the business, say this:

> "All discounts are approved through management. If you can help me out by letting me know what it would require to move forward, we can move forward today, and I'll do whatever it takes to get my manager to approve the discount."

From there, you'll go into a negotiation process landing on a number you both feel comfortable with. We'll discuss negotiation later, but this word track will create professional obligation to move forward with signed documents today. There is no more enjoyable form of professional obligation than signed documents. Once a prospect has done work to move forward with you, they will most likely become a client.

Visiting a referral source where you are looking to extract a referral, say this:

> "_____ (Networking Partner), I've been meeting with a number of clients that are signing up because of _____ (Value Proposition). I'm having a pretty slow month and could really use your help. Do you know of one client I could reach out to and discuss _____ (Value Proposition) with? It would really help me out to just have the name and phone number of one person I can reach out to. Is there someone who recently started their business that I could educate on this?"

Education

On any sales call, teaching the client something will create obligation. We'll hop back into a little more psychology here. Humans have a tendency to fear change. Fearing change is known as neophobia from a psychological definition. Explicitly defined, it is the innate animal behavior that retreats from an unfamiliar object or situation. With business owners wearing multiple hats, it is common that, if they are currently successful, there will be a risk to changing the status quo of their company.

Neophobia therefore becomes the primary reason someone will say no to you. It's just easier to not change things than switch to your product or service. "I don't want to learn a whole new system." This is the resounding phrase of a "no sale." Now that you know this is most likely your primary objection, it's time to make your prospects comfortable.

Whatever your product or service, it is your job to make your prospect believe it is "easy and user-friendly." There is no better way to do so than to tell them. Repeat it multiple times during your presentation. Make them believe your product or service is "easy and user-friendly" like the sky is blue.

But don't just tell your prospect. You must be eloquent and educated enough to show them how and why. You also need to make sure you're representing a product that you believe in. If you don't believe in it, you won't get your prospect to believe in it. I discussed this in the introductory chapter. If you do not believe in your product or service, you need to find a new lawn. Start there and come back to this book at a later date.

Educating your prospect is the fastest way to gain credibility and be seen as a business consultant. Also, because humans inherently fear change, you are able to use this to your advantage during the presentation. Instead of having your prospect fear the change of leaving their current product or service, you can educate your prospect to understand your product or service better than their current one. If you are able to do so, you will eliminate your prospect's fear of change.

I know you want to be the top sales representative since you are reading this book. In order to do so, you'll want another one of your goals to be the sales leader in knowledge of your product or service. Be a student of your craft, so you can soon be the teacher. Once you are the teacher, use education to create professional obligation for your prospects to sign up with your company.

There are a ton of other ways to create professional obligation through current clients, networking, and referrals. But I'll conclude this chapter as you now have the knowledge to greater understand these future chapters by comprehending how professional obligation helps create elite sales representatives.

Take five minutes to think about your current business. How can you immediately insert professional obligation into your sales calls? Before advancing to the next chapter, decide on three very specific scenarios that you will execute this week to prove the concept.

Ways to Create Professional Obligation in my Business:

1. _____
2. _____
3. _____

4

If You're Not Getting Better, You're Dead

Happiness is a relative term. Many people say they are happy when they are not. I think we're only truly happy when we are doing exactly what we want to do. My daily activities—living in Cyprus and becoming an author—are not for everyone. But human beings function on hope and growth. Learning a new skill and taking the next step in my sales and leadership career by writing this book is happiness for me.

My grandfather, Ken Markwardt, was the VP of finance for a Fortune 500 company. A lot of my business knowledge and work ethic can proudly be credited to him. Some people have professional athletes in their family to push them into sports and greater heroics at an early age and throughout their athletic careers. I was lucky to have business camp start at the age of five with countless stories and life lessons that I've taken with me throughout my entire career.

The first life lesson I remember learning from my grandfather at an early age was, "If you're not getting better, you're dead." It's an interesting concept that took me years to truly understand. And now I see it every day at every business in every city around the world. There are countless individuals who have no interest in getting better. They show up to their job with little dedication to doing anything other than playing on their phones and looking at Facebook.

I call these people the walking zombies of the working world. And in a weird way, we should appreciate them. Becoming elite would be much harder if half of your competition wasn't asleep. But they are. So, we thank them. If you are dedicated to getting better each day and put in a full day of work, you are already going to achieve more than 50 percent of the other sales representatives.

I'm staying at a little studio steps away—200 meters—from the sea in Limassol. And I did my homework to get here. I didn't rent a car, so taking a taxi would have cost me 60€ (US $75) from the airport. At that point, I may as well have rented a car. I researched a shuttle service online before I got here. From there, I talked to the tourism guy at the airport instead of standing there aimlessly as I waited for my suitcase. He helped confirm my first shuttle from the Larnaca airport to the city of Limassol. He even helped me figure out how to take a bus to the exact location of my studio from the stop on the shuttle. I made it twenty minutes later than a taxi would have gotten me there, and for only 9.5€ (US $10).

The point of the story is this: whether you are buying or selling, you will always make more or pay less if you do your homework. Homework pays off. There's a reason why the smart girl in high school went to Notre Dame and the party guy went to State. There's also a reason why the sales representative researching the company prior to the sales call has a higher closing ratio and higher revenue per unit than the other sales representatives.

In order to be the elite sales representative, you need to be the rep who does the homework. And when I say homework, I do mean at home. During business hours, you need to ask yourself one power question all day long.

"Is what I'm doing right now leading to my next sale?"

If it is not, do not do it. From 8:00 a.m. to 5:00 p.m. is the only time that you can be talking to someone who can buy from you. I am generalizing here, because I have done appointments at 6:00 a.m., 9:00 p.m., and even on Saturdays. My point is that if you start to replace your prospecting calls with doing research on the internet, your activity will go down. This is not the goal nor the point of this concept. Do your research after hours when possible.

The commitment to becoming elite is a passion, an excitement, and a fun adventure. You need to choose to have your laptop in front of you as you watch TV. When a commercial comes on, it's time for you to show your dedication to your craft. Even better, shut off the TV. The TV is not your prospect, but it is your friend. It's what the other sales representatives are doing in the evening. You are choosing to get better for your future appointments. You are choosing to make more money. You are choosing to become elite.

LinkedIn

Your first step in your pre-call planning homework is connecting to your prospects on LinkedIn. You should LinkedIn request all prospects prior to a sales call. If you aren't on LinkedIn, put the book down and sign up. LinkedIn is your online professional network.

The more connections you have, the more likely it is that connecting to your random prospect becomes a nonrandom prospect. It's likely they become a referral from the business you set up two years ago when you diligently connected with them prior to your sales call back then. I'll go further in-depth on referrals later in the book, but LinkedIn is an easy way to turn your random sales call into a referral from someone you know.

Please make sure you are ready to connect to your prospects. The obvious is sometimes the most important. You should have an updated photo. You should look professional, and it should be professionally taken. Dress the part.

Build out your business description, contact information, and website, add videos, and make sure you have been recommended and endorsed. The world is a somewhat predictable place. If I were to give you a birthday present on your birthday, you will most likely give one to me on mine. LinkedIn is the same. It's the social psychology of reciprocity. In other words, people often respond to a positive action with a positive reaction.

Endorse and recommend people whom you believe in. Once you've done so, ask them to write you a recommendation. It may require that you follow up with someone to get your recommendation, but you'll want to do so. It's worth it. As you connect to everyone on LinkedIn, you'll want to make sure you put your best foot forward.

If you connect to your prospect on LinkedIn and you have a mutual connection, your sales process is no longer with your prospect. Your sales process is now with your mutual connection. Your entire sales role turns into selling your mutual connection on calling, emailing, or in some way endorsing you to the prospect prior to your sales meeting. If a third party lets your prospect know it's the right decision to sign up with you and your company, this conversation will trump your entire sales presentation in a positive way.

Call your mutual connection. And definitely visit this connection when at all possible. Email should be a last resort. Your goal on the phone call or visit is to explain that you are looking to be endorsed to your now mutual connection. Maybe there is a "referral credit" you can offer them. Have them join in on the sales process and reward them for doing so. It's just as good as their bringing a random referral to you. In fact, it's even better. You're helping them as you help yourself. Being an elite representative allows you to find yourself helping people rather than selling them. And as a result, you help yourself to additional sales along the way.

Once they understand what you are trying to accomplish, and you have incentivized them, the plan is to have them make a phone call while you are there to endorse you. This is the best scenario. Countlessly, I have watched my mutual connection say these words:

> "Hey Susan. It's Tom over at Riley and Associates. How are you? Great. The reason I'm reaching out is that a good friend of mine, Jon Markwardt, let me know he's meeting with you on Thursday. I just wanted to let you know you're in great hands with Jon, and I've known him for years. I'd

recommend him to anyone and just wanted to give you the heads up that it's a great decision to work with him. Anyway, how's everything else at your business?"

The mutual prospect has no idea that I'm sitting there, and the phone is on speaker. But because I'm sitting there, my mutual connection says exactly what I need him or her to say as I hold my connection accountable. I've even written it out for mutual connections to read. It doesn't sound like reading over the phone, and we have fun practicing it a few times.

If you aren't around, the conversation will be much softer. I enjoy coaching my mutual connections on how to close. I always incentivize them to make the call. And my mutual connections love it. Even if you aren't in sales, everyone loves to close. Most people just don't know how. Once I've taught a mutual connection how to refer and close me, they're excited to do it again. And so am I!

The result when done correctly is the prospect will thank your mutual connection for calling them. Information is valuable. Therefore, the prospect is thankful for being given social collateral on your business. The result is a trust that helps the prospect move forward in their buying decision.

This golden ticket to your next sale doesn't always occur with every mutual connection. Sometimes the connection you share is not that strong or you may not even remember how you're connected to them. The elite will use this as a conversation and a path that you'll still want to go down. It shows just how well-networked you are as you let them know you share a mutual connection and you ask about their relation to the contact you now share.

If you connect to your prospect on LinkedIn and you do not have a mutual connection, this is still an opportunity to develop rapport at the onset of your meeting. Discuss where they went to college, former positions, mutual interests, and so on. This is an open invitation to gain trust from the prospect and earn their business by simply being better than every other sales representative they've ever met. Prospects appreciate your showing up prepared and caring enough to research their business.

If their LinkedIn profile is weak, you should help them. Social media is a vital marketing tool for all small businesses. If they are not on top of their social marketing game, they are losing business. Make sure you are connected to someone who specifically handles outsourcing of social media for businesses.

It's another opportunity to refer someone if they need or want assistance. The birthday present analogy goes a step further when you make someone else money. You will have the ability to call them out to return the favor. In my opinion, giving a referral is the equivalent to gaining a new sale.

From a preliminary standpoint, you should always be looking to sell every possible product or service you can to a business. You want to be their consultant and their trusted source for all of their business endeavors.

If you can't find them on LinkedIn, this also becomes a conversation piece. Earn their trust by becoming a business consultant and discussing the importance of their business's social network. This is typically an obvious one to refer, but it's also possible you just didn't find them or they haven't had time to create one. Have the conversation and you'll know if this is a referral opportunity or simply an opportunity to be seen more as a consultant. Either way, you are conducting yourself at an elite level.

Facebook, Instagram, Twitter

In B2B (business to business) sales, LinkedIn will always be first on your homework assignment, but your homework doesn't stop there. Social media is important to every small business, and likewise it is important to you and your pre-call planning.

All of the practices applied to LinkedIn can be applied to Facebook, Instagram, and Twitter. Please note, all of your profiles must be professional and a representation of you and your elite services. If they are not, you'll need to create professional accounts that you'd feel comfortable with all of your prospects seeing. If you have a Facebook account and you're chugging a beer in the photos, you'll need to keep that account as your personal account and switch your name so that only you and your fun-loving friends can view those pictures.

Protecting your online identity is extremely important. Prospects often Google who they work with. I had an extremely nice and talented sales representative work for me who had a poor web presence. She was targeted by one of her jealous friends on "The Dirty." For those of you who don't know, "The Dirty" is a website that spreads rumors about people as an open forum for anyone to post. While sometimes the stories are true, posts are often vicious lies trying to hurt someone. Unfortunately, when you Google her name, the first thing that appears is her article on "The Dirty." Although she has been able to overcome her bad web presence to still be extremely successful, she has had prospects point out the article and knows that it has ultimately cost her sales and credibility.

I once had an employee who was friends with me on Facebook post a picture of himself getting a tattoo during his "sick day." There's no reason to post certain pictures and say certain things online. Our private lives are no longer private when we post every detail on the internet for all to see. Posting the wrong activities can harm your credibility. But it could also cost you your current position, prevent you from getting hired, or even prevent you from dating the man or woman of your dreams by sending the wrong message about yourself. Don't let what you post on social media stand in your way.

Your Prospect's Website

Whether your prospect's website is average, under construction, looks amazing, or looks like something your five-year-old daughter could have designed, you need to look through their website and discuss it during your sales call. If you don't understand what they do, you'll need to Google what they do to at least get a baseline of knowledge. You can then discuss what they do without looking like the "other sales rep." If the website is remotely good, or you found anything slightly interesting, you need to compliment them on their website. This should be common sense, but becoming elite is thousands of little tasks that all seem like common sense once you practice them and gain results.

When beneficial to the prospect, this is a great opportunity to refer someone who does website design. The psychology of reciprocity goes a step further when you make someone else money. Remember, I am repetitive when I'm trying to make a point. As you hand out those birthday presents, remember, you will have the ability to request or strongly encourage that they return the favor because giving a referral is the equivalent to gaining a new sale.

I'm being explicit in how I am selling you throughout this book, so you learn to adapt and adjust your sales game. My goal is to be transparent on the process, be repetitive, and help you understand the execution of certain sales concepts. Effectively, you will execute them with greater confidence and enthusiasm. Being elite means knowing the how and the why.

When you've done a good job researching a prospect's website, and you can find a way to be sincerely interested. Start your sales call with this word track:

> "I enjoyed looking at your website and found your business to be very interesting. I've been looking forward to our appointment and was hoping to get a tour of your facility. Do you mind showing me around before we talk about _____?"
>
>
> (Your Company)

Obviously, this one will only apply to those who are in outside sales visiting the right type of business. But I can tell you that there is no better rapport builder than someone giving you a tour of their facility. As you walk around, begin your needs analysis on the tour. You'll develop a great connection with your prospect and have an extremely enjoyable start to your sales call on both sides of the fence as you walk around and ask questions.

When I first started selling, I met with a surfboard shaping company. James was the owner and an awesome guy. I was interested in buying a surfboard and extremely interested in how they were made. We spent forty-five minutes talking about surfboards and touring the facility. Our tour ended with James letting me know that he had a busy rest of the day and probably only had another fifteen minutes for me. I said, "No problem. I know this is the right decision for your business. I only need ten minutes to get you set up." James happily signed up with no sales presentation. He trusted me, and I'd established that I worked for a reputable company. Remember, the primary reason people buy is the salesperson.

Not only did I sign James up, but they custom built me a board at cost. In high school, my nickname was Starkwardt. My last name is Markwardt, and a good friend of mine, Nick Jacobson, switched the Mar to Star. For basketball fans reading this book, Stephon Marbury was called Starbury during his youth. Nick went on to a very successful collegiate career at the University of Utah and various professional teams overseas. As for me, my nickname in high school was the peak of my basketball career.

I took an entrepreneurship class at the University of San Diego, where I turned Starkwardt into Star Court. Star Court was an apparel company that I wrote a full business plan for. I made Star Court T-shirts, shorts, and even a commercial. The company targeted the basketball community and competed against Nike, Reebok, and Adidas in apparel and shoes.

Star Court never launched. In 2006, three years after I created my business plan, Starbury shoes launched and later became a full apparel company. The company still exists today. While I don't have a big apparel company, I still have my surfboard with my logo on it to remind me that you should ask for a tour of the facility.

Research Project

Research their business and the name of the person you're meeting with. Do a general web search on the person or company and then look for a recent article on their industry. If you search by the "News" search on Google, you may find a recent article that could have an impact on their business. If you find one, print the article to give them at your meeting.

In a best-case scenario, they will not have seen the article and you will immediately be seen as a resource for

"Sales Up Dude."

their business and not simply someone trying to sell them something. From a common sense standpoint, I'm sure you can already see the difference this will make in your sales call.

From a reality versus perception standpoint, you need to do this. When you see how it helps increase your closing ratio, you will make it part of your professional routine. It shouldn't be your exception if you want to be elite. It should be your rule.

I tend to point out the obvious as part of my guide to over-clarification and making sure you run in the right direction to become elite. But you are looking for positive articles. If you are meeting with someone in print media, you do not want to print out an article on how print media is dying and all of these businesses should close.

Preparation for Appointment

Now that you've done your research on the company, you are ready to make sure you have everything else prepared for your meeting. I always show up to get the sale. This means I come prepared and you will too. The more preparation you do to show that you prepared for the meeting with them, the more obligated the company is to sign up with you. I'm not referring to preparation for a meeting in general, but preparation for a meeting with the person you are specifically sitting down with.

Prior to my meeting, I consistently drop by a current client that is close by their location. If you can schedule the meeting, it's even better. My goal of visiting any current client is to up-sell or solicit a referral. The referral I'm asking for on this current client visit is very specific. I want to know if they know the prospect I am about to meet. If they do, I will use the same approach I use when I have a mutual connection on LinkedIn. When they don't, I'm still going to reference them as I walk in the door to my prospect. I use the following word track:

"Great to meet you, I was actually just visiting _____ down the street from you.
(Business Visited)
They've been a current client of mine for the past two years.

Do you know _____?"
(Business Visited)

We'll learn more about current clients in chapter 8, but this provides you with a good reference point on how to use them in preparation for your appointment.

Make sure you have a preprinted or electronic proposal. It should have the business name on it, the person you are meeting with, their phone number, and the quote. The quote should be for your highest revenue product. We'll be discussing this later in the negotiation chapter. For now, start making sure that your proposal is not handwritten. The client should feel as if you prepared specifically for them and did so prior to sitting in your car in front of their building.

Prior to walking into the meeting, you need to make sure that you are on your "A" game. Listen to your favorite song, walk yourself through the steps of your meeting, review your homework, and envision getting the sale. Every time you walk into an appointment, it is important that you adjust your attitude to believe that your prospect will be signing up. There is no one better prepared for this meeting, and you are the right decision for their business.

Elite sales, when done right, are half education and half performance. You need to make sure you perform as if you are on the biggest stage and all of your fans are watching. At this point in my career, I only enjoy selling when I bring sales representatives with me to watch. Part of being elite is not only performing well on the stage but wanting to be in front of a crowd. When you have a crowd, you will have more drive and focus on your actions. You are much less likely to skip a step when someone who you are trying to coach on doing things the elite way is watching.

Self-Evaluation

> **The greatest growth we achieve is when we realize the growth that we need to occur.**

The greatest growth we achieve is when we realize the growth that we need to occur. This allows us to focus on what makes us stronger. Elite representatives know what their strengths and weaknesses are. As a result, they have more opportunity for growth. Someone who doesn't know what they need to focus on does not grow.

All elite sales representatives know how to self-evaluate after their appointments.

"What did I do well?"

"What could I have done better?"

Until you are able to successfully self-evaluate, you'll need to call a mentor or your sales manager after each presentation and discuss those two questions. Always start with what you did well. You need to be proud of your skills and start there. It's always easier to give yourself constructive criticism when you embrace and celebrate the things that you are already doing correctly.

Even if you are at the point in your career where you feel as if you can self-evaluate, an effective mentor or sales coach will always provide an additional perspective that you may not have thought of. To truly expand your sales skills, you need to surround yourself with people who can help you grow and get better. Even Michael Jordan needed Phil Jackson.

Whether you got the sale or not, your sales call will not be done until you've met with the business on the left and right of your appointment. Whether or not you got the sale, you should have asked to be referred to both of these businesses. Either way, you have two cold calls to do before you can get on with your day. Try the following word track when you walk next door after your appointment:

"Hi, I'm _____ (Your Name) with _____ (Your Company). I just met with your neighbor _____ (Business Name) next door. _____ (Business Owner) is really nice and is taking a look at coming on board with _____ (Your Business). I just wanted to drop by to introduce myself and find out what you're doing for _____ (Product or Service)."

Regardless of their answer, your goal during this cold call is to set an appointment to come back and present. There is a comfort level that you just met with their neighbor and there is greater obligation to meet with you if they are on friendly terms with their neighboring business. Ask them to help you out and meet with you when you come back for your follow-up appointment with their neighbor.

Current Events

Embrace your nerd side. If you don't have one, get one. Be educated. Be interesting. Current events are interesting. And stories sell. You're selling yourself and your product with every story. As a general rule, you'll want to steer clear of religion and politics. As your second rule, make it your personal responsibility to know anything and everything that could or is affecting businesses in the United States.

If you are selling B2C (business to consumer), make it your personal responsibility to know all tax laws and city changes that affect the general public. If there is a tax law change, a tax credit available, a trend in a particular industry, or a general new practice that helps businesses grow revenue or reduce expenses, you are the source that your prospects and current clients can count on for this information.

With the knowledge you collect, you will want to make sure to get this out to your current clients on a monthly basis. I'll go into more detail later on how to effectively conduct these "monthly updates." For now, you should understand that this can and will be an efficient way to stay in touch with your current client base and solicit referrals. Use the following word track to follow up on a prospect that you have yet to close:

"Kelsey, I was thinking about you when I saw this article. I wanted to make sure you saw this as it could affect your business. I also wanted to follow up on moving forward with _____. I know we're the right
(Your Business)
decision for your company. I'll be in your area this Thursday afternoon. Are you free at three for us to talk about how _____ can help your business?"
(Your Business)

ABL

My grandfather has his own spin on ABS, and it's ABL—always be learning. Every profession requires ongoing education and continual development. The world is not a stagnant place.

ABL—always be learning.

You are reading this book and obviously care about your growth, development, and career. Congratulations! Caring is the first step. But there are plenty of relationships out there where people care about each other and their actions say otherwise. Caring about your career and committing yourself to self-development are two completely different things.

At the beginning of my sales career, I spent a lot of time buying lunches and beers for the top sales representatives that I encountered. I didn't care about their industry, color, sex, or creed. I was a nondiscriminatory elitist. If you were elite in sales, I wanted to talk to you. If you weren't, you were hurting my career. The first and one of the best ways to expand your knowledge is by surrounding yourself with people who are already doing what you want to do.

In order to fit in with your new crowd, you will now have to hold yourself accountable to a higher standard. By hanging out with anyone less successful, you will fit in easier. But your decision to do so will affect your ability to become successful.

I was extremely fortunate in how I entered my selling career. I joined the number-two team in the entire company. In order to fit in, I knew that I would need to be better than good. I loved the pressure that came with joining this elite team. And I love to think that I was the difference maker when our team finished number one in the company during my first year.

Once again, I probably need to over-clarify here. I've never been one to be rude or act as if I'm better than anyone. This is not a trait that comes with being elite. Sharing your knowledge and your skills is something that will actually make you perform at a higher level. I've been coaching for years and love it. It's why I wrote this book. But your time outside of business hours is your personal time. I encourage you to share your personal life with other successful people. You'll find the conversations to be more interesting as you and your friends silently and vocally push each other to be more successful in your careers and in life.

Surrounding yourself with the right people will immediately increase your sales skills. You'll swap war stories and best practices, but self-development is a process that you'll need to do on your own. Just as you have sales goals, you should have self-development goals. Start with what you are comfortable with and excited about.

I committed to reading one sales book and going to one seminar every quarter in my first year of sales. This felt like a big commitment considering how many hours I was working and my commitment to be the best. But I knew that I'd never be able to achieve my goals if I wasn't able to work smarter. Everyone has the ability to work hard. But working hard and smart is what makes someone elite.

As you work toward your goal of becoming elite, you should start by concentrating on working hard over working smart. Do your homework. It will pay off. I firmly believe that the harder you work, the luckier you get. I'm always willing to create my own luck. As you work hard, self-evaluate to get smarter along the way. You are getting better on purpose. Each day that you continue your development makes becoming elite easier and easier with every step you take.

As I conclude this chapter, please take a moment to write down your educational goals for my grandfather. He doesn't want you to end up dead, so you may as well get better. List at least three self-development goals.

Self-Development Goals:

1. _____
2. _____
3. _____

Be specific and provide yourself with due dates to hold yourself accountable.

5

You Jump, I Jump

I have zero directional skills. I will often use my GPS to go five blocks when I don't know where I am. However, in Cyprus, I do not have the luxury of GPS since I did not have a data plan on my phone during this time abroad. But I believe there is no better way to test my sales skills than to adventure for help without a GPS, a map, or the faintest idea of where I am at or where I am going. With full disclosure, I don't have the attention span for a map, and even when I use one, I typically do not end up in the right location.

I've been on the island at this point for almost two weeks. Through the help of numerous Cypriots and other travelers, I have navigated the island by bus everywhere from Limassol to the Troodos Mountains, to Paphos, to Larnaca, and to my location in Protaras where I currently call home. Each time I ride, my sales pitch is consistent to anyone who may be waiting at the bus stop, sitting next to me on the bus, and, of course, to the bus driver. I use my favorite sales word, help, and attempt to sell each of these prospects on becoming my personal tour guide to get me where I am attempting to go.

I'm sure that you're thinking the bus driver should be able to navigate me, but most of the time their English isn't that good and there are a lot of people riding the bus. I thought I'd sold one bus driver on helping me get to the Limassol castle during the third day of my trip, but he forgot to let me know when to get out. As I fumbled through a conversation with the person next to me, trying to explain what a castle was, I eventually realized that I'd missed my stop. It resulted in a one-mile walk backward. From this experience, it became my sales mission to sell two people on every bus ride. I would need to sell the bus driver and someone on the bus.

Failure

I absolutely love failing. And I encourage all of my sales representatives to fail. I can train, coach, and even provide you with an awesome book to read before you start selling, but I cannot prevent you from failing. You will make mistakes. No one is perfect. And no one closes at 100 percent. Not only is that okay, it's great! It's how we learn more effectively. When we fail miserably, our brains more accurately remember these times of failure than any ordinary event.

With great diligence and dedication to getting better, we prosper with every failure.

The best news about failing, besides our personal growth, is it provides us with pending leads to follow up on. If you didn't sell it today, there is always tomorrow. Top representatives know their closing percentage. If I close at 50 percent and didn't sell my last appointment, I can and should be confident that I'll get the next one.

Just as I'd finally figured out how to navigate the bus system in Limassol, I moved to Protaras, which is on the east side of the island. I'm sure I will be failing again. But this is what I do, and I'd yet to formulate a relationship sale from my bus rides. And I was determined to do so.

It was a beautiful Friday morning, and I woke up early to write at my kitchen table in my new and spacious apartment. After a few hours of writing, it was time for lunch. I went on my short walk to the sea and ate at the restaurant in front of a nearby bay. Afterward, I went down to the sea and snorkeled at the reef right in front of the restaurant. The fish, the sea, the air, the breeze, and the day provided me with a lawn that was getting greener by the day.

The only thing missing was companionship. When you travel alone, there's no one to comment on the things you are doing and your thoughts on the moment. I believe the secret to happiness is shared experiences, and, while I was enjoying my own experiences, I was getting tired of traveling alone.

I decided that I would migrate to the more populated Nissi Beach and try my sales pitch on the way to make sure I didn't get lost. With instructions from the bus driver, I sat down and looked out the window as I tried to gain familiarity with my new surroundings.

As the bus started to fill up, three women walked in that were stuck standing on the crowded bus. I moved over so someone could sit down. Anna sat down next to me.

"Where are you from?" I asked with confidence. I've stopped asking people if they speak English. I've been determined to just go with it.

"I am from Russia," Anna responded. I let her know that I was going to Nissi Beach, and, with great luck, she and her friends were headed in the same direction. Anna was extremely curious about why I had come to Cyprus. As I explained my story, she let me know that I could follow her to the beach. We got off the bus, and Anna introduced me to Stacy and Elena. I tossed my story on repeat as they asked about my travels alone through Cyprus. I joined them as we grabbed beers from a supermarket and headed down to the beach.

Nissi Beach has an island you can walk out to with an 8 meter (25 feet) cliff that many of the locals jump off of. I did it first and convinced Stacy and Anna to come with me a second time. Stacy was the first to go; Anna was a little scared after looking down.

I looked into her eyes and confidently said, "You jump, I jump." As I said it, I felt rather smooth. I didn't think there was any way she would recognize the line from the American movie.

But to my surprise, Anna replied, "Isn't that from a movie?"

"Yes, it's from *Forgetting Sarah Marshall*," I quickly explained with a straight face.

"No, I don't think that's it. Isn't it from *Titanic*?"

My *Forgetting Sarah Marshall* joke wasn't funny for her. I gave up. "Yes, I think you're right."

It turns out the iconic quote from *Titanic* was also known in Cyprus. And, unsuccessfully, trying to pass it off on a less-known movie did not garner a laugh.

Once again, you are probably seeing a theme here. I'm not very funny in any language, and the only language I speak is English. My jokes create more of a chuckle or a smirk even when they are understood.

It went as I said. She jumped, and I jumped right after. Having a shared experience together created a bond. That's why it is very important for you, as you attempt to create relationships, to get lunch, meet for happy hour, or go to an event. I once took a referral partner to opening day at the Del Mar horse races, and our relationship was forever changed. It's harder to not refer someone once you've shared an experience with them. Dale and I would always reminisce on the event, and it created an extended obligation for him to refer me.

"You jump, I jump."

The three Russian girls ended up being one of the highlights from my travels, despite the short time we spent together. I went out with Anna and her friends the next night; we all talked, partied, and drank. It felt great to have made new friends on my travels.

We met for another fun beach day the day after; then they were headed back to Moscow. Anna and her friends had provided me with new experiences and companionship for the entire weekend.

Sharing experiences with someone, whether for personal or professional reasons, develops relationships. I've stayed in touch with all three of them through Facebook and text messages. It also created more obligation, specifically for Anna, to spend more time with me.

"You jump, I jump" eventually turned into "You drink. I drink." And after a few drinks for me, "You dance. I dance." Not only does the shared experience bring you closer, it can provide you with your own inside jokes and a greater level of intimacy. As you look to develop your professional relationships, you need to eat, drink, and jump off cliffs together.

Remember, I tell multiple stories to get my points across and sell you on the concepts in this book. So let's migrate over to the business side of stories and say goodbye to my Russian friends. From a business perspective, there is often more persistence needed to create a "cliff-jumping experience."

While working in my first sales position, I was never required to have more persistence building a referral relationship than working with Emily and Craig in San Diego, California. The first time I met them, they literally asked me to leave their business. While this worked for the day, there is always another day and another opportunity.

Emily and Craig were providing my same service and looking at me as a direct competitor. While I technically was, I wanted to provide them with the opportunity to outsource this portion of their business, to grow their revenue, and to streamline efficiencies within their company. The problem is that they had no interest in talking to me, let alone jumping off cliffs with me.

As I continued to drop by with information and useful articles for their clients, I was warming them up to the idea that I wasn't a bad guy. I'd recently discovered that they were both active in the Chamber of Commerce, and there was a lunch event coming up in the near future.

I confirmed with the Chamber that Emily and Craig would be there. I finally had my opportunity to go "cliff jumping" with them (*even if it was a small cliff*). However, they had no idea that I would be there or that they would be jumping too.

It was an interesting event where the lunch featured a speaker that was talking about different tax laws that affected small businesses. After the event, I waited as people started to clear out, and I migrated over to Emily and Craig's table. I was determined to not talk about my company until we'd at least jumped in the water. We talked business tax law and about a conference that they attended in Las Vegas. Vegas provided us with a new topic to discuss as we got to know each other better. From there, I simply planted the seed of how working with me would generate more revenue and streamline their business. We were now on a different level, resulting from our time getting to know each other through the Chamber experience that we shared, so I was not shot down on the concept and my door would remain open.

During our talks after the Chamber event, I learned how much they were working and how their current processes really kept them captive in their office. Often times, businesses don't realize that outsourcing a product or service will most often increase their revenue. Time is the most valuable asset a business owner has, but they often discredit their worth by investing their own valuable time instead of outsourcing. Using their time in a different capacity will often generate more revenue for the business.

In this situation, not only would the increased revenue allow them to go on a nice vacation, but it would also provide them with a solution that could afford them a "vacation" every day from their current processes.

Exiting the meeting, I called my manager and asked for suntan lotion, vacation magazines, beach towels, and beach games to bring to Emily and Craig. I went into their office one week later with my presents, simply stating, "I'd like to buy you lunch and tell you more about how working with me will increase your revenue and allow you both to take a vacation."

The gesture of kindness worked, and they agreed to lunch. Having another cliff-jumping experience was exactly what we needed as things continued to move forward—as if it was simply a formality on both sides.

One of my largest sales came from developing a relationship—that initially didn't want to be developed—through a shared experience. "You jump, I jump" is a concept that can be taken to any professional setting with persistence and by finding the right cliff.

Never give up on anyone you're targeting. You need to have the attitude that everyone will be a sale for you. It's just a matter of time. I don't have "no sales." I have "pendings." While you never want to consistently hound your pendings to the point where you aren't developing new prospects, your CRM tool should never allow your pendings to die. Follow up efficiently and with appropriate timing. Eventually, you will find that if you conduct yourself as part of the professional elite, you'll get your prospects to take that leap of faith.

Just as I was able to have multiple experiences with Anna after our cliff-jumping experience, you too can create relationships that pay dividends to you throughout your career. After the initial conversion, I would continually take Emily and Craig out to lunch. We continued our friendship and our professional relationship, and I continued to get numerous sales from them on a regular basis.

You in essence acquire more than one sale every single time you build a new relationship. Just as rewarding, they will bring you friendship and true enjoyment from what you do. The sincerity of the relationship is as important as the sales you acquire. Many of the relationships I have in my professional career are relationships that I will take with me for the rest of my life.

Have Fun

You are in the amazing industry of sales. Enjoy it. I've often said, "I'm not sure what comes first—winning or having fun." Start having fun. It's part of how you build relationships. If you aren't winning yet, you need to enjoy the process along the way. You'll end up finding numerous people who want to join you for the fun. Worst-case scenario, you end up with some great stories to tell your friends as you truly enjoy what you do along your road to success.

Not everyone enjoys what they do. Take a minute to think about what a fun and exciting career you've entered and why you can truly enjoy what you do. Remember, part of joining the elite is being confident and happy with what you do. List three reasons why you believe sales is the right career for you.

3 Reasons Why Sales Is the Career for Me:

1. _____
2. _____
3. _____

Sales really is an amazing career. And as you develop your career, it can take you in many directions. Most CEOs have sales somewhere in their background because sales is the most important part of the organization. Without sales, the company cannot grow. If you've ever worked for a company where the CEO does not understand sales, you'll see how growth can be limited by your leader. Whether you have ambitions to become the CEO, or become one of the selling elite, there is no better position than a sales position.

Not only does sales set you up for success with multiple career paths to choose from, you're encouraged to go out to lunch, happy hours, and the Del Mar races to build fun and amazing relationships that you will have for the rest of your life. Take the time to enjoy this process and create your own stories along the way. Remember, stories sell. Until you have your own stories, "*Robin Hood*" stories from people you work with or from this book. Your story can be someone else's story by simply stating this:

"I read a sales book talking about traveling in Cyprus, and the author jumped off a cliff with a Russian girl quoting Titanic. You know, 'You jump, I jump.' It's a cool book and it made me want to travel and expand my sales skills. Have you ever traveled overseas?"

Let your conversation and story go from there. People love talking about traveling and their own experiences.

Whether you are formulating a relationship with a prospect, a current client, or a referral partner, relationship-based selling lays the foundation for effectively creating a referral-based relationship. Learning how to effectively extract referrals is the game changer for any elite sales representative. As we migrate into our next chapter on how to extract referrals, please take a moment to list your top three targets that you would like to create a relationship with.

Relationship Target and Activity:

1. _____
2. _____
3. _____

<small>Be specific and provide yourself with due dates to hold yourself accountable.</small>

6

Building Your Referral Army

The professional elite create an army of current clients, networking partners, friends, family, and even prospects that provide them with referrals on a consistent, yet random basis. The last chapter laid the groundwork for what I believe is the most important chapter in this book. Extracting referrals is an art, and, when done the right way, this art will expedite your quest in joining the elite.

In order to extract referrals, we look to the previous chapter to build relationships the right way. It is important to build relationships right from the start, or they will take much longer to build into a referral-based relationship.

One month into my Cyprus journey, I was still rocking the farmer's tan at the beach. If getting a full tan was my goal, I messed it up from the beginning when I was golfing in Minnesota prior to my travels. Anytime you do something wrong from the start, it will take much longer than if you started your process correctly from the ground floor. Eventually, I was able to break away from my Neapolitan arms, but it took a lot longer than I would have expected.

Properly extracting referrals is a seven-step process. You'll want to learn the seven steps and do them in the correct order. If you jump ahead, you will receive your proverbial farmer's tan. Eventually, you will be able to recover the relationship with persistence and an awesome attitude. However, I encourage you to formulate your referral army the right way and follow these seven steps as you build each relationship the elite way from the start.

Please note that I have met many good and even great sales professionals who only practice steps 1 and 2. If your goals stop there, you should learn how to grasp and implement steps 1 and 2 better than anyone else. For those of you looking to take your careers to the elite level, you'll want to learn all seven steps and practice them accordingly. Just like all of the other sales concepts in this book, you will not truly understand their effectiveness until you execute them and they work. Establish three referral partners and give yourself a timeline on getting through all seven steps of the referral process.

Referral Partner and Timeline:

1. _____
2. _____
3. _____

Step 1: Do a Great Job and Earn the Right

Our first step of the process is doing a great job and earning the right. No one refers someone who does a terrible job. When was the last time you had a bad meal and you told all of your friends to go to that restaurant? On the flip side, we often refer our friends without being asked when we have an amazing meal, see a spectacular movie, or travel to a unique location.

From a psychological standpoint, humans get great joy in being the "expert." Knowing something someone else doesn't know gives us a feeling of wisdom and understanding. As we learned earlier, humans genuinely want to help other humans. Therefore, to some extent, all humans enjoy educating each other. Not only is there benefit to helping someone with a referral or signing up for your product, there is benefit to referring a friend to an awesome product or service. It's fun to have your friend call you after they go to the movie or restaurant you recommended and thank you for referring them to an amazing night out.

Therefore, sales professionals who do an excellent job will naturally get referrals. It will happen just because you've done a fantastic job. Business owners and consumers like to refer their friends and family when they have received amazing service. They will want their friends and family to work directly with you. If you've only done a moderate job, but they love the product or service, they will simply refer the product or service to their friends and family. There is a certain level of obligation to make sure they refer you directly when you've gone the extra mile for them.

By earning the right, you've created an obligation for them not just to refer your company, but to refer you. You have helped them, and now they will want to help you. Once again, they receive physical and emotional benefits from helping you. It is the "helpers high" concept we learned in chapter 3.

Step 2: Ask for Referrals

A number of sales representatives who earn the right do not ask for referrals. They actually rely on the hope strategy. Hope is not and will never be a sales strategy. While doing an outstanding job will get you referrals in many cases, it is your job to ask for those referrals as a true sales professional. It can be as simple as saying,

> "I rely on referrals to grow my business. Who do you know that could use my services?"

This word track is the softest way to ask for a referral. It simply plants the seed. Most of the time, business owners and consumers will say they need to think about whom they know before they refer. As a result, referrals are another opportunity where it is important for you to be repetitive. When you are doing a great job or know you will do a great job, you are able to let them know early on that you rely on referrals for your business during your sales presentation. In other words, during your presentation to a prospect, you might say this:

> "As a result of the awesome service at _____,
> (Your Company)
> I am able to rely on my current clients to refer a large portion of my business. The average current client refers me to at least three of their friends. Do you know three businesses you can refer?"

You will want to smile big after this statement. While the question is confident and sometimes seen as an aggressive statement, you can smile and laugh to soften it up. Most of the time, the prospect will smile or laugh and respond, "I'll have to think about it." Most importantly, the question plants the idea of referring early on. You would then go on to explain your referral program, if you have one. If you do not, you should create one. It's worth a $25 gift card for your current clients to join your army of referral partners. (Please note, higher revenue sales may require a larger incentive, or simply going the extra mile with step 1 may be more appropriate depending on the company or product.)

Remember, asking for referrals is not one and done. It should be done repetitively until you get a referral. If you are doing it the right way and are professional, you will have people apologize to you along the way if they haven't provided you with a referral yet.

Step 3: Extract, Give Examples

Not everyone can think of what you are looking for off the top of their head. Providing the person you are soliciting for referrals with examples allows you to give them a very specific person that they may know. "Do you have anyone you can refer me to?" most often leads to, "Let me think about it."

The more specific you are on the referral you're looking for, the more likely it is that you will get a referral that truly benefits your business. This concept applies to almost anything. At a restaurant, you may ask the server to recommend a dry, white wine that is semisweet. You're more likely to get the type of wine you want over simply ordering a white wine. When you extract your referrals, it is important that you get specific about what will benefit you the most.

These examples may apply to your industry:

1. Do you know anyone who recently started a business?
2. Do you have any friends or family members who recently got married?
3. Do you know anyone who is concerned about saving the environment?
4. What business owners do you know that aren't very good with technology and could benefit from my easy and user-friendly service?
5. Who are the other business owners you work with?

Write your top three referral extraction questions specific to your business.

Referral Extraction Questions:

1. _____
2. _____
3. _____

You'll want to ask at least three questions to get their wheels turning. Let them know you are trying to help them think of someone as it would really help you. If they are not able to think of someone or say they need more time, just set a follow-up time they agree on to collect your referrals.

Step 4: Get the Name and Phone Number

Often, the client will say that they will have someone call you. Waiting for that person to call you is another hope strategy. Professional sales is not sitting by a phone, hoping that it will ring. When they let you know that a referral will call you, you will respond with the following word track:

> "Often, referrals forget to call. And I won't. (Smile.) I'd appreciate being able to call and introduce myself. I'll simply say, 'Hi, this is _____ (Name) with _____ (Your Company). _____ (Referral Contact) referred me to you as my service will benefit you and your company. I'm calling to set an appointment with you, so I can explain why _____ (Referral Contact) thought we should meet.' If they aren't interested, I will not push for the appointment since you referred me to them. If they are interested, I'll set an appointment and tell them more about _____ (Your Company)."

Telling your prospect what you will say on the call provides comfort that you aren't going to make them look bad or be pushy when talking to their referral. The word track does not sound "salesy" at all. Especially the last part where you let them know you will not be badgering their referral. You won't have to. When they hear that someone they know is recommending they talk to you, it forms an extra layer of obligation for them to meet.

Step 4 is all about making your client feel comfortable and excited to provide you with the information you need to make your next sale happen. Make them feel comfortable and you'll get their referrals and phone numbers every time. It's important that you make them feel good about your reaching out to someone they know and putting their approval on your doing so. If they do not want you to use their name when you reach out, you've received instant feedback that you have not done your job in making them feel confident about your product or service and how you conduct yourself in earning the right.

Step 5: Get Them to Call Their Referral First

We learned about this concept in chapter 4 when we discussed mutual connections on LinkedIn. Remember, I will be repetitive with concepts that I think can truly grow your business. The likelihood of getting a sale from your referral is three times more likely when the person referring calls the prospect first, compared to just providing you with a name and phone number. It is also the primary reason why many sales representatives give up on asking for referrals. They get to the point where they are receiving referrals but are not closing a high percentage of these prospects. They lack full names, phone numbers, and this vital phone call. As a result, they end up looking at referrals as something that costs them time rather than makes them money.

The donkey will run much faster for the carrot over the stick. Humans are the same way. We all love rewards. Incentivize them in some way to work for you. Remember, the incentive is sometimes to simply help you because you helped them by doing such a great job with step 1.

"Even the Cyprus Donkey Loves Incentives."

Be explicit on why the phone call is so beneficial to you. Let them know that by having them do the calling, it makes your job so much easier. Often I use the following word track:

> "Just so I don't sound like a crazy person when I call, it would really help me out if you could call _____
> (Name of Referral)
> and give them the heads up that I'll be calling. It's much more likely that they will take my phone call and sign up with _____ if you call."
> (Your Company)

Once they understand what you are trying to accomplish, the plan is to create a conference call or have them make the phone call while you are there so they endorse you. This is the best-case scenario. Countless times I have watched my current client or networking partners say these words:

"Hey, Sandy. It's _____ over at
                        (Referral Contact)
_____. How are you? Great.
    (Referral Contact's Business)
The reason I'm calling is that I'm going to have a friend of

mine, _____, reach out to you for
              (Your Name)
_____. He works for
          (Product or Service)
_____ and has been extremely
        (Your Business)
helpful for my company. Whether you end up using him or not, I'm confident that you'll benefit from a meeting to hear about his company. Anyway, how's everything else at your business?"

Step 5 is a game changer in the referral process. And as you can see here, the word track is slightly different than when I introduced this concept previously. Please adjust to your industry and comfort level, but make sure you apply this sales concept to effectively change how you are referred. Once you've accomplished step 5, you'll never want to get referrals any other way. You'll find that your referrals are stronger, your closing ratio is higher, and you're no longer selling. You're simply reaching out to a new friend with a great product or service as you grow your professional relationships. Everyone wins!

Step 6: Hold Them Accountable to Refer

Whether you have received a referral during your referral extraction or not, the follow-up is equally important for getting the referral. If there is something pending, you'll need to establish a time when you are following up to check in on their referral. If they want to call their brother (step 5) later that day, you will let them know you'll follow up at a set time and see if they were able to talk to their brother.

Let them know you'd much rather confirm they were able to connect as opposed to blindsiding their referral. If they need time to think about whom they can refer after you gave them multiple examples, you will follow up with them at an agreed-upon date. If they want to use your service prior to referring, you'll use the following word track:

> "No problem. A number of my clients prefer to use our service prior to referring me. I'm confident in our service and know you'll refer me once you've tried us out. So, I will plan on following up with you in thirty days to make sure you are enjoying the service as I promised you would. I'll be looking for three referrals when I follow up as long as you are a happy customer. Is that fair?"

When they say yes, you'll need to add it to your CRM tool. Some of your telemarketing will actually convert over to referral collections. Make sure you collect on the hard work you did to get your referrals. You deserve them!

"Trick or Referral!"

These follow-ups should all be done over the phone or in person. However, current client follow-up should not be limited to just a phone call. You'll learn more about working your current clients in the upcoming chapters. But I'll elaborate here that everyone should be working their current client base on a consistent and automated basis for referrals.

Step 7: "1 Referral, 1 Sale, 1 Favor"

This phrase was my mantra in my chase to become part of the professional elite. I believed this was all I needed to be successful. Please allow me to explain.

As you can see from my first six steps, I believe that you need to be diligent on doing whatever you can to obtain at least *1 referral* from your networking target. Once you've obtained that referral, you need to do everything possible to turn that referral into *1 sale*. It's why step 5 is such an important part of the process as it increases your closing ratio. You must obtain the sale just as I discussed in step 1: do a great job and earn the right.

Once you've obtained your referral and gotten your sale with a happy new client, your job in step 7 is to ask for 1 *favor* from the person you were referred to. They will typically be hesitant when you ask for your favor until you explain. But once you explain, the percentages are high that they will do your favor without any follow-up. Here's the word track for your favor question:

"I rely on a large portion of my business to come from _____. I really appreciated
(Referral Source)
_____ referring me to you.
(Referral Contact)
The best way that I can thank _____
(Referral Contact)
is by really taking care of you. As long as you are happy with my services, could you help me by thanking _____ with a short email or a quick
(Referral Contact)
phone call for introducing us and let them know you are happy with the services I provided?"

Almost everyone will say yes if you have done a great job and earned the right with step 1. And more than half the time, they will send that email or phone call without your even following up. If they do not, it's very easy to ask them a

second or third time by simply asking for their help and letting them know that it would mean a lot to you. Make sure they understand how much you appreciate their doing so and that it really helps you. The reality is, it does.

As promised, I will be explicit if the large light bulb for this concept has not gone off. Effectively what happens in this scenario is the professional equivalent of what happens when you recommend an amazing restaurant to your best friend. Your best friend calls you up and thanks you for your recommendation, and you feel even more confident on referring that restaurant to more of your friends. So you end up doing exactly that.

People love to provide referrals that others enjoy. You are effectively making them look and feel good by doing step 1 as they refer you. You've effectively helped their business and now their friend's business. While they may have been hesitant to open up their rolodex to you before, the "favor" call has now made it okay to do so. Your referral army now grows exponentially by your first soldier and now your second.

This chapter explains the best possible way for you to grow your business with referrals. Following the seven-step process will not only gain you more business, it will allow you to work smarter and more efficiently as more and more people start "working" for you. It is a crucial chapter that will most likely be worth a second read for those of you who want to become a referral champion. But for now, let's take one last look at the seven steps prior to moving on to chapter 7.

1. Do a Great Job and Earn the Right
2. Ask for Referrals
3. Extract, Give Examples
4. Get the Name and Phone Number
5. Get Them to Call Their Referral First
6. Hold Them Accountable to Refer
7. "1 Referral, 1 Sale, 1 Favor"

Learn each of these steps and please make sure you do them in the right order. I'd hate for you to waste unnecessary time on the beach trying to fix your farmer's tan. Elite sales professionals have a process that can and will be respected by those you encounter. Just as it's impressive to watch an elite athlete in their element, everyone appreciates someone who is exceptionally good at their craft.

As you excel at the referral process, make sure those referring you see your professional actions along the way. You'll want to update them with any status change and properly thank them whenever you sell one of their referrals. Dare to be better than everyone else at the referral process and commit to excellence. This chapter will be a big part in your quest for becoming elite.

7

Just Say No

As I discussed in the introduction, this book was written to help you grow into an elite sales professional, so I won't be covering how to handle basic prospecting calls and standard telemarketing word tracks. While this is required in any sales professional role, I will do a deeper dive on prospecting for the elite.

What you will learn about prospecting for the elite is that there is *always* a reason for making a call. You are calling on purpose with a specific action item to engage or reengage your prospect at a level that other sales representatives are not doing.

Not only does this alter the call, it provides the business owner or consumer with the directness necessary to not waste their time. By simply stating, "The reason for my call is _____." you've eliminated the frustrated prospect question, "What can I do for you?"

We learned earlier about the importance of a CRM tool and following up on something personal, like a Minnesota Vikings win, or professional, at a specific and agreed-upon timeline. You must have a follow-up agenda. This chapter deals with creating new and unique reasons to follow up or contact someone for the first time.

My travel prospecting has had me diving in the trenches to meet new people on the bus, the beach, and the restaurant. In all of which I am selling to expand my knowledge of the island, to get navigational directions, and add fun experiences to my travel. However, I was much more strategic with my prospecting prior to arriving on the island.

A friend of mine from high school in Fargo, North Dakota, is half Cypriot. Christina visits the island once or twice a year and could provide me with a much larger sale than any of the random people that I would prospect on the island.

Like any elite salesperson, I utilized the resources of my internal network. If you aren't willing to sell to your friends and family, it means you are embarrassed about what you do. I'm proud of my position as a traveling salesman and author. While Christina and I hadn't talked in a couple of years, we arranged for a phone call prior to my trip. She provided me with specific points of the island to visit, foods to try, and introduced me to a number of her friends and family via Facebook that I could meet along the way.

Not only that, it turned out she would be in Cyprus during the time I would be here. Christina was one of my biggest sales during my travels. And it resulted from prospecting on purpose with a reason for my call.

I met up with Christina on my travels and was introduced to her cousin, Athena. Athena lives in Nicosia and promised to meet up with me in the city when I made my visit to the capital. My intimidating Nicosia travels turned into advice on where to go and time spent with a born and raised Cypriot. I also met Christina's boyfriend, Oryan, who was a really cool and interesting guy from Israel. And all of a sudden, I had a new group of friends on the island that resulted from prospecting I'd done months ago. Strategically prospecting Christina allowed me to reconnect with a friend and provided me with a sale that upgraded my travels to a new level of comfort in a foreign land.

As you take a hard look at how you are currently prospecting today, it is important that you think in terms of how you will differentiate yourself from every other sales rep out there. And along the way, think about what you have right in front of you that can help you prospect in a smarter and more efficient way. The goal is to work the combination of hard and smart to be elite. Let's take a look at a few things that are right in front of you every day.

Facebook

Just as Christina was able to help me, you have friends who are willing to help you. But you must be willing to ask. If you are not taking advantage of your personal social network for prospecting, you are missing out on numerous sales. Your social network is *your* network because they already know and like you. It's much easier to call upon your friends and family because there is already an established obligation for them to help you.

It is possible your friends and family will de-friend you if you are posting a work-related message on a daily basis. But you are doing a disservice to yourself if you are not posting something at a minimum of once a month and a maximum of once a week in your personal circle.

Your social network is valuable, but it is only valuable if you take advantage of it. Be proud of your company, your position, and the help you are able to provide to your friends and family with your product or service. Referrals from friends and family close at a much higher percentage with an additional layer of integrated obligation.

The primary reason why sales representatives do not utilize their personal network is that they are embarrassed about what they do. I've heard numerous sales reps say they don't want to sell something to their friends or family. If this is how you feel, you will never be elite. The dedication it takes to become elite requires you to be proud of what you do.

We learned earlier that it's important to have fun and enjoy your position. Now we take it a step further as it's important to be proud of what you do and share that with the people closest to you. Please repeat this power statement and don't move on until you believe it like you believe the sky is blue and your grass is green:

> "I am proud to be in sales and want everyone to know what I do for a living."

As a new sales representative of any company, your prospecting should begin with those who are closest to you. There is no better presentation than presenting to someone who has an obligation to watch you fumble through your presentation. These presentations will not only make you better, but often the obligation of being your friend or family member extends to the prospect buying.

Google Alerts

I think we all have certain things we are constantly watching for and alert our attention to. I'm a huge Minnesota Vikings fan, so if I hear something on TV or radio about the Vikings, it will stop me in my tracks. While I was in Cyprus, I found that running into other Americans just doesn't happen. In some ways, it would be a lot of fun to connect with someone randomly from the States who has also traveled all the way to this foreign land.

As a result, I never jumped up so fast as the day I was back at the beach and saw this girl wearing a stars and stripes, Fourth of July bikini. I couldn't believe it. It was still July, and I thought it was awesome that she was representing our country so far away from home. I jumped in the water and walked out to her, her friend, and the guy that I presumed was her boyfriend. I didn't care. I figured they were all American, and I was excited to talk to them.

I ran up and said, "Hey, where are you from?" With anxious anticipation of a California, Texas, or a New York answer, I got the blank stare that I often get when someone doesn't speak English. I know that I must have turned completely red as I sheepishly continued to speak after no response. "Ummm. Do you speak English?"

She responded, "No. Sorry." Her friend spoke broken English enough for me to explain that I thought she was from the United States due to the bikini. I guess the girl had no idea and just liked the pattern. She pointed to the guy in a blue swimming suit and told me they were from Greece. I think they were mocking me, so I'm not really sure where they were from.

I felt dumbfounded. I didn't know whether to say the pledge of allegiance or go back to my towel. Actually, I knew exactly what to do. I went back to my towel with my red face. I laid down and decided to not make a fool of myself for the rest of the afternoon. I have not chased down anyone else when I see this US alert. Apparently in Cyprus, it's just a pattern.

Alerts create action in professional sales. When you search out a proper alert that affects your business, the alert will hold you accountable for great activity. As a result of committing ourselves to continual growth and education, elite sales representatives jump up from their beach towel for google alerts and news on small business law changes, industries, and specific companies they may be targeting.

In chapter 4, the importance of researching companies and industries prior to your new prospect appointments was discussed. What we now learn about prospecting and reengaging "no sales" is that this research should actually be ongoing. And when it is, the search for additional articles and pertinent information is always accessible for your immediate prospecting and weekly appointments.

The fastest way to automate this process is to add industries and business names to your Google alerts when you do the initial research for an appointment. As almost everyone uses Google every day, this is literally a prospecting tool that is two clicks away from effectively changing the way you prospect on a day-to-day basis.

By enabling a Google alert to notify you of new articles as they occur, you automate this process and search element. This way you are not constantly searching for top companies that you are targeting. When a new article comes out, you now have a reason for your call. You should congratulate them on their latest article or press coverage or provide them with industry-important information as you follow up.

This best practice becomes very apparent when you are on the other side of the interaction and you know what the sales representative is doing. I've had many sales representatives contact me to sell me on their product or service. While I'm always aware that they had simply set up a Google alert for my name or the company's name I was working for, I always replied to emails discussing a particular article they knew mattered to me. Their dedication to being different and elite grabbed my attention and resulted in additional interaction. While it didn't necessarily mean I would be purchasing their product, they were earning the right as they built their credibility.

It truly is important that you actually read the article and personalize your message. If you do not, you are like every other sales rep out there who learned how to set up a Google alert. As part of the elite, you truly need to care about your prospect and their business. This interest in their general well-being will take your career to new levels.

Local Advertising

You should know and be on the lookout for any and all free media that you can find local business advertisements in, such as a weekly business journal. They are all around your neighborhood grocery and convenience stores, and all you have to do is pick them up. If there is a free magazine or newspaper that businesses advertise in, you read it. Some people clip coupons to save money. You clip articles and advertisements to make money.

Some people clip coupons to save money. You clip articles and advertisements to make money.

Save the article or advertisement clippings in your car. As an elite representative, you still realize cold calling needs to be a part of your business. But why cold call when you can warm things up? You've now generated reasons to walk into these businesses with a unique attention grabber.

"I was really excited to see you in _____.
(Name of Media)
(Hand the prospect the article or advertisement.) I was in the area and wanted to introduce myself as my top clients understand the value of marketing and PR exposure."

If a business is advertising locally, they are looking to expand and grow their business. As a result, they are well versed in their determination to grow revenue and minimize costs. Your product or service should provide them with one of these two solutions the business is looking for. And you've immediately found a unique way to prospect the business. Here's your telemarketing word track:

"Hi, this is _____ with
(Your Name)
_____. The reason for my call is I
(Your Company)
recently saw your advertisement in _____.
(Name of Media)
I am reaching out because I work with many businesses

in your area. I would like to discuss a free marketing program that I provide my clients and how my business can effectively help your business."

Monthly Update

If you are in B2B professional sales, you are in the business of helping business owners generate more revenue and reduce costs. As a result of being an elite sales professional, you come across more business owners and consumers on a weekly basis than in any career position out there. It's what you do. Your job is to be interacting with prospects on a daily basis.

Use this to your advantage and the advantage of the business owners you interact with. As you provide your monthly updates (email newsletter) to your client base, you should highlight one of your current clients as free marketing inside the update to feature their business in two to three sentences.

They will have two requirements to be highlighted in your monthly update:

1. The company must be a current client.
2. They must offer some type of coupon in the update.

You are effectively now targeting businesses that are paying for advertising and providing them with free advertising. Encourage your current clients to share the coupons with their employees to effectively reach thousands of people through your distribution. It's important that you maintain the credibility of your monthly update by only providing great deals to your clients and highlighting the business in a short paragraph like this:

"This month, we highlight _____
(Business)
in our current client spotlight. As a current client of
_____, they are offering a
(Your Business)
discount to other _____ clients to
(Your Business)
take advantage of their _____
(Product or Service)
at a discounted cost. Please see the attached coupon and feel free to share with your employees."

You can personalize the item with one or two additional sentences. But you'll want to keep it short. This way your monthly update on useful information doesn't turn into spam for the business owner. Your monthly update not only provides marketing for one of your clients, it now offers a perk to your clients receiving the email as many will take advantage of the coupon you are able to provide.

As additional businesses take advantage of your free marketing program, you'll want to print the coupons and examples of your monthly update emails to show on your presentations. You will find that a number of businesses will sign up for your product or service to take advantage of your free marketing as much as they are signing up to take advantage of your product or service. You are prospecting in an entirely different way by providing value that does not inherently come with your product or service. You are selling yourself as a better solution and someone who can impact their business.

The reality is that many businesses don't know if their marketing dollars are an expense well spent. If you are able to provide them with any type of free marketing to reduce the cost of their current marketing budget, you are reducing their costs and providing them with a reason to sign up for your services.

Make sure you spotlight the right clients that provide something your other clients could use and enjoy. It is even better when the offer is something they can forward to all of their employees. Effectively, this compounds the number of people you are able to reach with your marketing efforts to provide additional value to your current clients as you grow your business.

The Power of No

There isn't a word out there that can gain your credibility stronger during prospecting than saying the word no. In sales, we are often trained to say yes and find a way. The reality is that always saying yes is not possible. All businesses and people have limitations. People buy from honest people whom they trust.

When you are prospecting, you may need to handle a quick-fire objection asking if you do something that isn't possible. You should quickly respond you do not and provide an alternative option when available. Let the prospect know that you would never tell them you can do something you can't. Respond with sincere honesty:

> "My product can and will benefit your company, but this is currently a system limitation we do not handle. I am always honest with exactly how and what we can do for your company. I'd like to meet with you next Thursday at one to show you exactly how _____ can still
> (Your Company)
> benefit you and your business. Does that time work for you?"

While this is how you want to handle this objection, the most profitable place for saying no during your prospecting is when the prospect is requesting an appointment that doesn't fit in your schedule. You need to respect your own time. In order to do so, you are not able to have one appointment on one side of the city followed by another in the opposite direction. This doesn't make sense, and you need to say you are not available. It will cost you activity and money if you do not respect your own calendar. Work your territory and your position efficiently. Schedule the appointment when it works best for you.

To do this, you should operate on a consistent schedule. This will give you strategic control and constantly allow you to know your general availability. I operate on the nine, eleven, one, and three model. This allows me to schedule up to four appointments a day with time for a quick lunch in between my appointments.

I control my schedule. If someone requests a 10:00 a.m. appointment when my entire day is wide open, I still say no. I would let them know my only availability is at 9:00 and 11:00. In situations where my set times did not work for the client, I made an exception to this rule and let the prospect know I would be adjusting my schedule for them and in order to do so I'd be looking to move forward on doing business together on our appointment. This trial close establishes any objections the prospect may have early on and lets you know how serious they are on moving forward.

You will find that when you respect your own time and manage a busy schedule, you immediately appear more elite. Prospects don't want to sign up with the sales representative who can take an appointment at any time on any day of the week. You've instantly become more attractive with greater credibility by simply managing your schedule and respecting your time.

As you say no and negotiate a time that works for you and the prospect, you should only be giving two options. It's known as the either-or close. As you do, you'll want to continue to be stubborn, so you don't bounce yourself all over the place and the appointment times are comfortable for you to have a productive and efficient day. Never reveal your calendar is wide open. You have a schedule and you are scheduling your appointments appropriately.

> "Does morning or afternoon work better for you?" Morning response. "Okay, great. I'm just looking at my calendar, and I have a nine and an eleven on Thursday morning. Do either of those times work for you or should we look at a different day?"

This is much different than, "What time works for you?" Or, "No problem. That time works for me." It's not your job to instantly respond that you are always available. Control your schedule and say no when you should.

The other sales representatives sound desperate if they are saying yes to every appointment. If the prospect is only willing to meet if you can swing by for fifteen minutes on their lunch break, they are not taking you seriously and don't respect you. Do not commit to showing up to this appointment on a day where you are not in the area. You'll still want the opportunity to sell them on more time and what you have to offer, but do it on your schedule and don't waste your gas money when you aren't in their area anyway. You'll swing by at noon when it

"Just Say No."

is efficient for you. If you don't have something scheduled in their area, schedule this appointment one to two weeks out and schedule all future appointments in their area on that day as well.

Prospect the "Right" Prospect

From the concept of saying no, we take it a step further in order to truly understand who your prospects are. If you are able to establish that someone does not have the potential to buy, do not waste your time. There are often system limitations that prevent the sales process from moving forward. Take notes in your CRM tool and have a way for tracking that system limitation, should something change at your company. This will allow you to target those people right away when the change occurs. An example would be an insurance agent that does not offer a line of insurance the prospect is looking for. Once again, please make sure you have a system to collect this data with the ability to run a report. These system limitations are your future sales when your company expands the product or service.

Language barriers can often get in the way as well too. If you can't understand each other, you aren't going to be able to sell your prospect. If you have a language specialist in your company, you should always be willing to pass the prospect on to the representative that speaks the same language. It's the right thing to do for the prospect.

However, it's important to note that you shouldn't immediately run away when someone doesn't speak your language. You've already made the phone call or shown up for the appointment, so you'll want to quickly establish if there is another way to communicate and win the business. Often there is someone else at the business who can converse with you.

Along my travels, I have found myself in numerous situations where the language barrier prevented me from any type of sale. There was no greater language barrier than the Russians who rented the place next to me during my first stop in Protaras. However, through broken English and an app on their phones that translated what we were each trying to say, I became friends with four wonderful people on holiday who had all the patience in the world for me.

One evening, we drank until the late hours of the night, passing the phone back and forth between us as we laughed and understood each other in a whole new way of communication. Thus, you shouldn't immediately give up when you have something preventing your sales process from moving forward. Always ask those two to three additional questions to either establish your need to move on or figure out another way of moving forward to get your sale.

As we advance into future chapters on current clients, lost clients, and negotiating the business, you must note that prospecting never goes away. You are continually prospecting some type of sale no matter whom you are targeting. It is important that you always understand your objective in all of your sales activities. If you don't know your objective, your activity is merely an activity as opposed to a calculated sales call. Be calculated and be elite on purpose.

8

The Front Line of Your Referral Army

I now have an unofficial office on the east side of the island. Just steps from my apartment in Protaras is a small café that is part of the Cavo Maris hotel and overlooks the sea.

Each morning, Michalis, my new friend, brings me my frappe the way I like it—with two sugars and a little milk. Michalis is a local Cypriot and my current client. Cypriots are a warm and inviting people who want to share their culture, learn about your travels, and help you enjoy their island. The people of Cyprus make the island beautiful just as the Mediterranean Sea makes the beach refreshing.

Each day, I look to sell Michalis on teaching me more Greek words and reviewing the words I've learned. Today I learned, "Kaliméra fíle mou." This translates to "Good morning, my friend." We're getting more complex from hello and thank you. I also look to him for referrals on places around the island that I should visit. It's great to get a local's perspective on where I should go and what I should do.

Having Michalis as a current client is much different than cold calling a random person on the bus or at the beach. Michalis already knows me, understands my story, and wants us both to have a pleasant experience as we interact each day. Yesterday, he referred me to Cavo Greco as a place to adventure on my scooter and detailed two spots that would be exciting and photograph-worthy. Not only did he give me details on the experience, he also provided me with a warning on snakes that are in this area and where not to go.

Referrals from current clients always save time. In the professional setting, we've already learned that referrals, when done the right way, close at a higher ratio. You will save time getting to your next sale. In the personal setting, I will save time by not having to go to the hospital because of a snake bite!

The best news is that current clients naturally and on purpose attract new current clients as well. My grandfather once told me that when you don't know what product or service to use in business, you should choose the product or service that everyone else is using. Numbers don't lie.

Pascal works every day with Michalis and became interested in me and my story as well. He eventually introduced himself. All Cypriots are fascinated by why someone from San Diego, California, would be living in Cyprus. As a result of the two-day travel to the island, Cyprus does not get many American travelers. I've been told by a couple people that I may be the only American on the island.

In my travels, my product is myself, and I am being presented as unique and different. It is extremely important that you present your product or service in a matter that differentiates you from your competition. People buy when they are genuinely excited about what you are selling. With genuine excitement, the conversation on price disappears. It's no longer about the cost. It's about receiving a product or service that their business needs and effectively makes their life easier. This allows them to generate more revenue and provides a solution for a specific need.

For professional sales, there are two reasons to visit current clients:

1. Upgrade their account with additional products

2. Solicit referrals

You should do both on every current client call. Elite sales reps know their objective when they are on a sales call or visiting with current clients.

Because visiting current clients is a metric that most sales representatives are asked to follow, you will find weaker sales representatives walking in without an objective. Their objective may be to visit their new friend to talk about a football game or drop something off. While they may feel as if they are performing a sales activity, they are only building a relationship that they are not capitalizing on. Sometimes it is appropriate to just do step 1 from chapter 6 as you build the relationship, but if you never move to step 2, then you're just hanging out.

Upgrade Their Account

Whether it be from an email blast or walking in with the specific intention of talking about an additional product, you want every current client to be using every product or service that you offer. The more products you have wrapped around the client, the less likely it is they will leave. Maintaining their current client status is vital to them being a part of your referral army. Lost clients do not refer.

In order to upgrade their account, you will need a current client appointment. All appointments should have a set agenda, so that you can maintain your objectives while you are there or on the phone. After building rapport, use the following word track to set your agenda:

> "Just to set the agenda of our meeting today, we'll be spending fifteen to thirty minutes together depending on questions. First, I want to find out more about your business and how _____ (Your Company) is working for you. If you have any questions, concerns, or feedback for me, I will make sure I get the right person involved to service your account and answer any questions you may have. Next, I have an update for your business on _____ (Educational Value Point). I'll then be discussing some additional products that may be a good fit for your company. If they make sense for your business, I can get them started for you right away. Finally, I do rely on my current client base for referrals. As I mentioned on the phone, I have a great current client program that I want you to take advantage of. I'll be looking for three referrals and will ask you for those at the end of our meeting. Does that sound like a fair agenda?"

I've never had someone object to my agenda. Once in a while they may tell you they're tight on time. In that scenario, you'll want to move straight to a product you think you can up-sell them on or just hammer them for referrals. Elite sales representatives understand their objectives and are adaptable to each one of their appointments. Let's go through the components of a current client meeting.

Timeline of Meeting

Everyone is busy. If you don't let them know how long you will be there, they will spend the entire meeting looking at their clock wondering how much time you are taking out of their day. Business owners wear many hats, and consumers don't have all day to sit around and listen to your sales pitch. Always estimate the meeting time on the low end. If you properly engage your prospect, the additional minutes will no longer matter as they will be excited about what you are presenting.

Feedback on Service

You need to let your client know you care and want to help them with their account if there are problems. If they are experiencing excellent service and are completely happy, they are now an ideal candidate to write a testimonial letter. When a happy, current client can't make a phone call to your prospect for you, it is important you have testimonial letters on hand to show prospects they should have confidence in your product or service.

The elite always have up-to-date testimonial letters that cover multiple situations they could incur as they meet with prospects. When you have an established relationship with a current client, it is always best if you let them know what you are looking for. Remembering that everyone is busy, you could even offer to write a sample letter that they could change or alter to their comfort level prior to putting it on company letterhead and signing it. In order to receive a testimonial letter, you'll need to have done your job earning the right.

If you have earned the right, and they agree to the testimonial letter, it is like everything else in sales. You'll need to put it in your CRM and follow up until you get it. Getting the testimonial letter is effectively a sale. This endorsement will be a difference maker with some of your prospects who are on the fence. Being elite means doing things that indirectly increase your closing ratio.

On the other hand, if the client is experiencing problems, you'll need to be straightforward that you are not the right person to service their account. If there is a problem with their account, make sure you get the short version. You don't want to spend thirty minutes listening to them complain about a service issue that you are unable to directly assist them with. Save time by letting them know you wouldn't want them to explain their story twice and you'll have a supervisor call them today.

If it is an extreme situation of bad service where you can't move forward with your agenda, call a supervisor from the service side of the house and put them on speaker. Have the client explain the situation and, once you are off the phone, immediately move to asking for referrals. You will no longer be worried about upgrading their account. You can touch on the additional products briefly. But people do not buy when they aren't happy. However, now that you've shown them the level of service you bring to the table, you will want to exploit this for referrals.

> "I know you've had some problems with _____, but I hope you can see the
> (Your Company)
> level of service I bring to my clients. I will give you my personal cell phone number so you can call me at any time if you have any future problems. I want you to get the service you deserve. In exchange for my work and dedication to your account, I rely on referrals to grow my business. Do you have one name and phone number I can reach out to? It would really help me out and allows me to greater service my current clients as they help me grow my business."

If you are intimidated by giving out your personal cell phone, you aren't thinking about things correctly. I would rather take one five-minute phone call at nine o'clock on a Saturday night and get a referral than continually be telemarketing and chasing down new business on my own. I want my current clients to work for me; therefore, I always follow step 1 in gaining referrals. Earn the right. Create the obligation. Build your referral army!

If you ever have someone inappropriately use your cell phone number, you should never think this is acceptable in your quest to become elite. You can either text them that you will block their number if they can't maintain a professional relationship or immediately block them. Being elite does not mean you need to compromise your personal safety or comfort. You can always find a better soldier to join your referral army.

Update for Business

Establish yourself as a business consultant. As I discussed in chapter 4, it is important that you are constantly seen as the expert and stay on top of current events. Using Google alerts keeps you on top of their industry and company.

This portion of the meeting is where you update the client on a tax law change or something that they should know as a business owner or consumer. Maybe there is a minimum wage change for your state, a worker's compensation law change, or a new tax credit they may not know about. It doesn't have to be something new for the general public. It could be a website

"No Referral Too Small."

design change to your product or service. Make sure you update them on something as you grow your credibility.

Doing these things will establish your care for the client and gain their trust. They will buy and refer more when they trust you and see you providing additional value to their business. These types of updates should go out en masse to your entire current client base. Make sure you send a monthly email as discussed in the previous chapter to each of your current clients.

Once again, it should provide them with valuable information, and the last line should remind them of your current client program for referrals. If your company does this, great. If not, start your own. I strictly use a monthly email for this and label it monthly update. If you send your updates more often than once a month to your current clients, it will increase the number of "unsubscribe" responses.

At my first company as a manager, I used to research topics and send an email to all of the sales representatives in Southern California as a best practice. I would randomly get emails from around the United States that someone in another state was using my monthly update. These were smart and elite sales representatives who, at some point, got on my distribution list for the email or someone else's current client email list in Southern California. As a result, they were able to work more efficiently as the email and research was done for them.

Work efficiently and *Robin Hood* great sales practices whenever you can.

Consequently, I've taken this same practice to each company I've worked at and have watched sales representatives experience success at every place it has been implemented.

Additional Products

It may sound silly, but you need to know what products your current client is using prior to your call. Many sales representatives actually ask the current client what they are signed up for. Whether they say it or not, the client is wondering how and why you don't know.

Your presentation should be formulated from the products they don't have as part of your homework the night before. Use the following word track as you present the additional products:

"I was surprised to see that you weren't using _____. Most of our clients take
(Additional Product)
advantage of _____ as it provides
(Additional Product)
_____."
(Value Proposition)

You'll then want to navigate into all the details of the product, additional value propositions, and the cost. Go through each one of the products with the same level of detail as you would to a new prospect you are presenting to. If they are not signed up for numerous products, you will only want to present a maximum of three, unless they've shown interest or committed to a greater amount of time for your appointment.

Ask for Referrals

This portion should be very assumptive. Remember, the key to obtaining referrals is being repetitive. You should have planted the seed on your phone call when you set the appointment, reminded them in your confirmation email, mentioned referrals as you set the agenda, and asked at the end. So they are expecting you to hit them up for referrals on the appointment. Follow this word track:

> "As I've mentioned before, referrals are extremely important to me and my business. I appreciate you referring me to anyone who can benefit from my services. I ask each current client to provide me with three names and phone numbers for me to reach out to. Do you have those available for me?"

Whether they give you one, none, or three, you'll want to extract more after they think they are done referring. Always get more. It's much easier to get that additional referral from the person who is already referring than it is from sitting down with a whole new current client and starting a new agenda all over again.

If they can't think of anyone, or if they can, you should always ask them to walk you to the right and left of their business. Some of the easiest sales I've ever had were a result of the business owner introducing me to their neighbors. When they don't know their neighbors or are hesitant to do so, you'll walk next door anyway. Do not leave until you talk to the neighbors.

Essentially, current clients become part of your referral army, whether they refer you or not. You'll be walking next door regardless if they refer you. I like to refer to my current client base as "insta-referrals." If I'm ever in need of an immediate referral, I can always go visit my current clients.

As you make your current client visits, you'll want to work them strategically so your next touch with the client is more efficient than your first. If they aren't on your distribution list, make sure you get their email address. Add them the same day, so they don't get lost in the one thousand and one things you are doing to be elite. If you have any reason to follow up to collect your referrals, add the follow-up call to your CRM tool. Elite sales representatives follow up diligently to get the result they're looking for on everything. Don't miss out on a referral because you were too lazy to schedule your five-minute follow-up call or email.

While the elite will typically use their monthly spotlight opportunities to gain new clients, it can also be used to provide leverage for your current client base to give you referrals. You can make an additional requirement to be featured in your monthly update by requiring three referrals to receive the free marketing for clients that are already established with your company. Remember, this is your monthly update in which you are providing value-added information to your current client base. You get to make the rules.

When Should You Visit a Current Client?

Positioning a current client call is most effective when done in the same location and just prior to a new prospect appointment. While we discussed this earlier, I will reiterate that visiting two current clients prior to your appointment with your prospect in the same area will positively impact your business. Not only will you be able to reference the current client visits as you build rapport, but it is possible the business owners know each other. As a result, your current client visits may result in the current client being a reference to help you sell your prospect.

Current clients should be an important funnel for you in your quest to become elite. Not only are they already sold on you and your company, but they can also be worked smartly and efficiently to help you grow your business. There are numerous ways to have fun with your current clients through referral contests, testimonial letters, and expanding your relationships around your territory.

The top takeaway from this chapter should be how to effectively and efficiently conduct a current client meeting to upgrade their account and solicit referrals. As you take your current client game to the next level, you will need to build out your current client distribution list. You will need to send a monthly update email every month. And you'll want to incorporate follow-up calls into your telemarketing time to collect referrals from your current client base. Current clients are the fastest way to vastly expand your referral army. They're already with you, now get them to work for you.

Prior to moving on to chapter 9, please list three new current client programs that you will implement with an accountability timeline. Be creative. Design the best program for your particular product or service and have fun implementing it.

Current Client Programs:

1. _____
2. _____
3. _____

Be specific and provide yourself with a timeline to hold yourself accountable.

9

Your Fallen Soldiers

I treat lost clients the exact same way I treat a current client. The only difference is, instead of looking to upgrade them, I'm looking to bring them back to my product or service. They already know your product or service, so the goal is to narrow in on what they liked about your product or service and understand what it will take to regain their business.

It is important that you are direct while talking to lost clients, whether in person or on a telemarketing call. You are specifically looking to find out two things:

1. Why did you leave?
2. How can I win you back?

If you've ever wanted to get back together with an ex-girlfriend or boyfriend, you know that the conversation will typically be about what has changed. If both parties feel that something has changed and there can be renewed confidence in the relationship, the couple may reunite. In the same manner, you are looking to reengage your relationship with your lost client. They have either now realized what they are missing out on, or you'll be required to show them how your company has effectively changed.

Most of the time, the reality is that current client loss occurs from lack of education. They do not completely understand your product or service, and if they are unable to get the assistance to solve their problem, the current client leaves. Often the client leaves without even asking for assistance because the new solution appears faster and easier. This becomes the ideal opportunity for you to be the expert and educate them on why they should not have left in the first place.

Elite sales representatives are always the most educated sales representatives in the company. Transforming yourself into a professor of your company allows you to come across as a business consultant, not just another sales representative. All elite representatives are seen as consultants.

As a result, you are able to provide better service because you care to do so. Your prospects sign up with comfort and confidence, and your lost clients return with renewed belief in the company. The primary reason someone will buy is the sales representative. In many ways, they are buying *you*.

Lost clients can effectively be worked prior to a new prospect appointment the same way that you would work a current client. Instead of mentioning to the new prospect that you were visiting a current client, you would say this:

"I was just down the street visiting _____.
(Business)
They recently left _____ and
(Your Business)
are looking at coming back."

This statement is entirely true; they are looking at coming back because you walked in there. But please note that professional sales means that all of your statements should be honest statements. I repeat. You should never lie, exaggerate, or guess an answer to get a sale. Credibility takes a long time to build and only seconds to ruin. The key to being part of the professional elite is building an army of people who trust and rely on you. The dividends from your army will pay a far greater reward than any one-off sale you may get by making up a story.

Prospects may ask why the lost client left when making this statement. You should be brutally honest. We will however use some common sense here. If the lost client down the street was a train wreck, it is best not to mention that you were visiting them. In most cases, you'll feel comfortable letting them know the problems they had. Go on to tell them why those problems won't occur with you if they sign up. But also let them know this:

> "No one company or person is perfect. As a result, I believe great service occurs when you have problems. The primary reason my clients love me and my company is how quickly I help them out if they ever have a problem. All of my current clients have my personal cell phone, and I answer it at night and on the weekends if they call. And if I don't pick up, I always call back."

It really is a very small thing to be willing to answer your phone for your clients. But it ends up being a value proposition about you. You'll need to explain that you are often the wrong person to be calling, but you will always be happy to refer them in the right direction. You should explicitly let the prospect or client know they are welcome to call if an emergency does occur. But be very specific so you do not turn yourself into a customer service representative.

All of my clients knew that my direct role was upgrading their account and reaching out to their referrals. They knew I was in sales because I was proud of my position and I was explicit with exactly what I do to avoid confusion. They also knew that if it really was an urgent situation that I'd be happy to take their call and get involved.

Most people feel much better in any situation if they know that someone cares and is available for them to find a solution. Contrary to popular belief, blowing off steam does not effectively make people feel better. It actually just fuels the fire to blow off more steam unless you are provided with constructive steps to a solution. Make sure you are providing them, in one way or form, next steps to a solution, even if that is getting someone else to call and service their account.

Sigmund Freud believed that pent up aggression or anger is like a boiler that would burst if you didn't let out some steam. New studies have proven it acts as more of a drug. Letting out the aggression feels good. So continued anger and aggression tends to follow.

The best way to deal with an enraged client is to let them know that you will do everything in your power to help provide them with a solution and not engage in their anger. I repeat, do not engage in their behavior if they are angry on the phone. You will hurt your credibility, and, from a psychological perspective, it will effectively worsen the situation. Keep repeating that you will get a supervisor involved as soon as possible and you will do everything in your power to solve their issue.

With angry phone calls, you need to get off the phone as quickly as possible. They are not leading you to your next sale. Let your operations department fix the problem and make sure they follow up with you to let you know when it's been fixed. When it is fixed, you've earned the right to ask for a referral and a testimonial letter.

Sales is a science, after all, and if you study it correctly and understand human interaction in the sales process, it is much easier to operate as one of the professional elite. You're not just doing it because you read the techniques in a book. You're doing it because you understand the importance and psychology behind it.

A lost client agenda should be different from your normal sales presentation. Set the agenda with the following word track:

"Just to set the agenda for our meeting today, I know that you already know a lot about _____.
(Your Company)
As a result, I'll keep our appointment under thirty minutes and highlight what's changed. First, I want to start by getting to know your business a little better and the needs of your company. I'd also like to find out what you liked about _____ and what caused you
(Your Company)
to leave. After this I'll inform you on what's changed since you left and address whatever caused you to leave. I'll break down the pricing and will be giving you a great deal to come back. At _____, we are
(Your Company)
disappointed when a client leaves us, and I'll do everything

in my power to get you back. The sign-up process will be quick and painless, as we already have the bulk of your information. Does that sound like a fair process?"

Once again, they will typically say yes. In some situations, you will find out immediately that the only reason they left was price. In my professional experience, one out of four business owners make more than half of their business decisions with price as the determining factor. If they are looking at your business as a commodity, they will strictly be looking at your business as an expense. It is vital to your sales process that you are able to distinguish yourself from your competition and help your prospect understand the value that comes with your company.

You will run into prospects who refuse to see any type of difference and keep coming back to the price. In this scenario, you should hold your ground that your current clients have chosen your company for the different value statements that you reiterate. Sometimes though, the only way to get the deal will be on price. I discuss this more in the next chapter on negotiating. However, it is important to understand, once again, lost clients do not refer.

Units refer. Revenue does not.

If you are really stubborn on not going to your maximum discount, you could end up missing out on a sale; sales can provide referrals. To be elite means you are gaining every possible sale you can in order to build your referral army. If it becomes necessary to give that large discount, do it. Just make sure they understand you are doing it because they are a lost client and get something in exchange. You'll need at least one referral from them to provide the discount. Always give a reason why you are giving the discount and hold them accountable to growing your business. You've just given them a present with the large discount, so it's only fair that they return the favor.

"No Referrals Left Behind."

Be Adaptable

Throughout my travels, I have encountered situations where I did not understand a single word that anyone around me was saying. While I couldn't understand what was being said, I still understood what was going on. Everyone comprehends laughter or a raised voice. We say as much with our tone and body language as we do with our words. Although it is hard to participate in the conversation when I do not speak the same language, it draws attention to one of the most important concepts in being elite. You must be adaptable.

Lost clients will often require adaptability to close the business and this skill may be necessary to not annoy the prospect. Remember, they already know a lot about your company and have used your company before. You'll need to be watching for verbal and nonverbal cues to gauge their interest in your presentation. It is quite common to over-present to a lost client where you should be concentrating more on rapport and what's changed.

It is important to recognize when someone is in a hurry or wants to spend additional time with you for a more detailed presentation. Most of the time, you will have verbal recognition as you set your agenda on the meeting time to know how much time is comfortable for your prospect. However, it is still important to watch body language and their tone throughout the meeting.

FULL SPEED AHEAD

If your prospect is looking around the room, seems distracted, or is providing you with short answers to your needs analysis, you do not have their attention and you are on a shot clock. Speed up your presentation and get to the meat and potatoes of what you have to present. You can slow down and provide greater details once you sell them on providing you with more time. Your entire sales process has changed based on the body language and tone of your prospect. When your prospect is in a hurry, you are no longer selling to get the sale. Your objective is now to sell the prospect on being excited about one of your value propositions to give you more time. Without the additional time, you won't be able to earn the right to win their business.

DROP ANCHOR

If your prospect is asking a lot of questions, sitting back in their chair, or has let you know they've been looking forward to the appointment, you are able to go more in-depth throughout the presentation. It's time to educate your prospect on the bells and whistles of what they have been missing out on and what has changed since they left.

Your meeting location provides clues as well. If they've brought you into a conference room over standing as you present, you are able to adjust to the presentation they are looking for. It's great news when you are being given the additional time, but you need to use it effectively. Your objective is to educate your prospect on your benefits to create obligation to move forward as you close the business.

By spending the additional time with the prospect as you accomplish your first objective of getting them to move forward, you are well on your way to earning the right in adding them to your referral army. I would always prefer one long appointment where I am able to wow and educate my prospect over three quick appointments where I need to spit out my value proposition without establishing rapport and educating the prospect. The goal is to drop anchor, educate, win the business, and earn the right to extract referrals before you leave.

Mirror Your Prospect

It's part of the subconscious, but humans are often attracted to people they feel a connection with. It's the old saying, "Birds of a feather flock together." The psychological concept behind this is known as similarity. It means that humans often have an innate and genuine connection with those who are similar to them.

When I visited Makronissos Beach, I found white sand and amazingly clear water. It was somewhat similar to many of the other beaches I'd visited in Cyprus, but each new beach felt as if I were looking at a new postcard of somewhere I'd never been before. It appeared to be a beach more for the locals to enjoy rather than some of the more touristy beaches in front of the hotels.

As I jumped in the water or sat down by someone at the beach, I tried to talk and meet new people. It was a particularly fun part of my travels as I enjoy these random conversations with each new prospect I meet. However, that day, I was having a particularly disappointing experience as I seemed to be striking out with everyone I talked to. No one spoke English.

I decided to migrate to a new area of the beach. As I was walking, I heard two girls speaking in English. I excitedly and loudly exclaimed, "You speak English!" I'm sure they thought

I was weird. I must have been gaining a reputation as the weird American on the island. They were from London and energetically talked to me about their travels and inquired about mine as well. On a beach where not many people were speaking English, we formed a connection by speaking the same language.

I'm sure you realize that you aren't going to have a new best friend just because you speak the same language as your prospect. However, the point is worth making. We often find new best friends at a bar cheering on our mutually favorite sports team. Your closest friends may come from activities or organizations that you've been involved in. Or maybe your significant other is someone you met while doing a shared interest or being at a specific event.

You don't need your prospect to be your new best friend, and I'm not suggesting you lie to connect with your prospect on similar interests. Lying is not for the elite. The psychological concept of similarity provides additional insight into making your prospect comfortable and earning the right by mirroring them throughout the presentation. If they are leaning forward intently, you should lean forward. If they are sitting back relaxed, you should sit back as well. Do your best to mirror the speed at which they are talking and provide them with the comfort that you are both on the same team.

No Problem

No matter the situation, it's not a big deal. In sales, we are not doctors and no one will die. While everyone wants to feel respected, someone's lack of respect doesn't constitute clearance for you to provide the same. Prospects who take a phone call during a meeting, show up late, or miss the meeting should not feel bad for their behavior.

I discuss this now as you'll find the lost client that was only willing to give you fifteen minutes may often cancel, be a no-show, or be late for your meeting. While you will maintain professionalism, you should not let your prospects cost you money. Use the situation to create additional obligation to move forward without making them feel bad.

You also have an opportunity to do something else. Treat the opportunity with an awesome attitude. Never take a canceled appointment as an opportunity to derail your day. Be adaptable and quickly switch your activity. After all, there are one thousand and one things you could be doing every day. Pick something else and be productive. Your objective becomes to adapt quickly and continue to search for your next sale.

Never wait more than fifteen minutes for a prospect who is late unless you've touched base via phone and have agreed to the new time. As you wait, cold call the business to the left and right or tackle a few phone calls or emails. There are many other activities you could be doing. This being said, you should be careful about going back to a prospect who has missed your appointment. Try the following word track when someone misses your appointment:

> "No problem on missing our appointment. I can tell you're very busy and wear a lot of hats at your business. My schedule is busy as well. So I just want to make sure if we reschedule this appointment that you'll be available to move forward with _____."
> (Your Company)

This trial close will allow you to see how serious of a prospect you are dealing with and know if it really is worth rescheduling. If possible, try to get the prospect to come to your office for the second appointment if you are in outside sales. This commitment to come in your direction only creates additional obligation for their time and energy spent to move forward. If they aren't very serious, you'll want to reschedule the appointment more as a drop by when it fits into your schedule and you're in the area anyway.

Well-Rounded

The number-one reason people buy is you, and it's even more apparent during your lost client appointments. They've already made a decision to leave your company, and it will take some convincing to get them back. The rapport throughout your presentation is extremely important to win their business.

Sadly, not everyone wants to talk about the Minnesota Vikings with me. It's important that you are able to have rapport in conversations that allow you to connect with more than one type of personality. Often you are able to look around someone's office and have a decent understanding of how to connect to your prospect. When you aren't sure, you'll want to be able to talk about things that are interesting to most prospects. *Hint on the number-one answer:* your prospect is always interested in talking about their own business. Make sure you do your homework.

I am typically able to build rapport and talk to most prospects about the following topics:

1. What I learned from my homework on their business (Ask for a tour of their business as you discuss.)

2. How I know our mutual connection (when applicable)
3. Current events (especially events and topics that affect their industry or business)
4. Traveling (Most people have traveled somewhere.)
5. I was a camera man for the San Diego, Fox 6 Nightly News. (Most people watch the news and are interested in what happens behind the scenes.)
6. I am originally from North Dakota. (Everyone is from somewhere. My hometown of Fargo is unusual.)
7. I was the coach of the University of San Diego water-ski team. (Many people enjoy water sports. And once again, something unusual.)

Did you notice weather did not make the list? You can definitely start with weather, but you're better than that. It's hot in Cyprus during August. I never understood the point of this conversation when someone wanted to discuss it being hot here. They brought it up, and I confirmed. I could also confirm the sky is blue, but I'd rather talk about something with more meaning and have a real conversation. It's one of the many things I do on purpose to make sure I water my grass to make it green.

Unless there is a blizzard or hurricane taking place, I think we can do better than talking about the cold or warm air you experienced as you walked from your car into their building. Also, if there is a blizzard or hurricane taking place, it's a good day to cancel your appointments. Being elite doesn't mean you prospect during hurricanes.

"Unusual Weather We're Having!"

You'll want to keep numbers 1-3 on my list for your own rapport-building topics. But it's also important that you have your own topics (4-7) to connect with your prospects. Please think about what personal conversations are unique to you in order to connect with people through the concept of similarity or general interest and note them now.

Rapport Topics:

4. _____

5. _____

6. _____

7. _____

As we start to look at the many avenues of growing your business, you can start to see that operating at an elite level does not constitute one task or activity. While I note chapter 6 where I discuss referrals is the most important chapter, all of the chapters are extremely important to understanding the world of elite sales. The reality is they all tie back into creating your referral army. Working smarter and growing the people working for you will provide you with a lifestyle that you'll be proud to have built through your hard work and dedication to doing your one thousand and one activities at an elite level.

Prior to moving on to our next chapter, it is important that you continue to build things in the right order. As you grow in your professional career, it is initially more important to grow your new clients, current clients, and lost clients into your referral army instead of doing a skilled job of negotiation. Your referral sales will be much easier to negotiate.

Concentrate on adding current clients and lost clients to your weekly activity. Schedule one current client or lost client appointment prior to each one of your scheduled appointments next week. Make sure you use the agendas laid out in the last two chapters and walk in with an objective. Elite sales representatives do everything on purpose. Being elite is not an accident. Choose to be elite and schedule your current client and lost client appointments for next week.

Did I sell you on completing the activity? I was direct. I provided value statements of what you would receive. I was repetitive, and I told you stories to sell you on the concepts and the point of the activities. Like any sales pitch, I won't bat 100 percent, but I'm happy to go down swinging.

10

The Negotiation Battle

I believe in two rules for negotiating, and I practice them whether I am buying or selling. While I was in Limassol, I wanted to go into the Troodos Mountains and visit the Kyykos Monastery along with the many villages in the mountains that have amazing food and rich history. The city bus system wouldn't get me there, so renting a car was the recommended option for exploring on my own.

I talked to three different car rental companies, but there was not much room for negotiation. So I walked away all three times. It was easy for me to walk away. I knew the mountains were winding roads. I have no navigational sense as noted earlier. The cars have me driving in the American passenger position, and I'm supposed to drive on the wrong side of the road. This had all the makings of an unfortunate car accident.

I researched an excursion company that would tour me exactly where I wanted to go for less than the price of the rental car. There was zero need to negotiate as I booked my trip. Chris came to my exact location with a small shuttle bus and picked me up for the excursion. He spoke fluent English, was very knowledgeable of the island, and provided a tour of places that I would have had an extremely hard time navigating to on my own.

Chris announced there was a trip to Paphos the next day and anyone on the shuttle would get a discount for booking their second excursion. I was extremely appreciative of Chris and everything he did for me on this excursion, and I hadn't been to Paphos or the west side of the island yet. But I felt confident that I could navigate myself there by bus if I couldn't negotiate a great deal with Chris. Everyone likes a great deal, but I absolutely love getting great deals. It's a fun game for me. I want to know that there is no one else getting a better deal. Let the negotiation begin.

And to do so, let's take a look at our two rules for negotiating:

Rule #1: Whoever sets the bar wins.

Rule #2: You have to be willing to walk away.

I needed to negotiate without anyone else around for the optimal discount. I would wait until I had Chris alone to attempt to get the best deal. The 5€ ($6 US) discount he initially offered put the trip at 30€ ($36 US). I would be happy to pay 25€ ($30 US), but, anything more, I would walk away and attempt to navigate the road to Paphos on my own.

At our last village stop, I was able to set the bar. "Chris, I'm on the fence for the Paphos trip. I'll go if you can do the trip for 20€."

Chris laughed and responded, "No, there's no way I can do it for that price. 5€ is the discount I can give you."

"Meet me in the middle, Chris, and I'll do 25€?"

Chris held to his guns and explained that if he did it for any less than 30€, it would have to come out of his own pocket. Interesting—the entire shuttle was at the basement price and I couldn't get it any cheaper.

Sticking with my second rule, I walked away. Walking away often results in getting the deal at the price you've held to. If I'm buying, I need the person selling to really want the sale. If I'm selling, I need to be 100 percent confident that the person really wants to buy.

In this scenario, I'd just walked away from my easy and enjoyable trip to Paphos, and Chris didn't flinch. He let me walk away. I now had challenges in front of me to get there, and it would most definitely take longer. Remember, in life, you will typically get what you pay for. As a result, you always get an option. Do you want a great price or do you want great service? I'd just signed up for a great price, but I would not have the luxury of Chris navigating me anymore.

In the process of our excursion, I'd made another friend, or proverbial current client as I'm calling them in this book. I'd developed a relationship with Chris and appreciated all of the insight he gave me on the island. He had an answer for nearly all of my questions. I truly hoped at some point that I'd see him again. The island has a little over a million people on it and many more during tourist season, but in some respects the island is small. As we drove around, Chris seemed to know everyone as he waved and greeted people wherever we went. He explained that this was the Cypriot way; they all knew each other and were friendly.

I set out on my bus adventure to Paphos with non-buyer's remorse. I wasn't totally sure where I was going, and I could end up spending my entire day not seeing the locations I wanted to get to. Worse, I may never make it there. However, with my usual sales tactics to get other people to navigate my way, I was sitting on a bus to Paphos and later on Aphrodite's Beach on the west side of the island.

As I took photographs of one of the most beautiful beaches I've ever been to, I felt pretty accomplished by doing the trip on my own and without the help of Chris's excursion. I ate my victory lunch overlooking the beach and went down to sunbathe after my meal.

Enjoying the sun and the sea, I spent some time on this amazing beach before realizing that I needed to move if I wanted to see anything else. This was the easiest spot to get to via bus, and travel was about to get complicated from here. While I felt good about what I'd done so far, it sunk in that, in all likelihood, I'd waste the rest of my day trying to see just one more location on the west side of the island. I walked up to the bus stop and looked at my watch; I had ten minutes before the bus arrived. I decided to go over to the souvenir shop to entertain myself until the bus came. As I walked over, Chris greeted me with a big smile and shook my hand. He was here on his tour.

Chris was very surprised that I was here and wondered how I had made it to the west side of the island. When I explained that I took the intercity bus for 7€ roundtrip, he laughed as I could tell he was impressed that I'd found a way to do my trip cheaper than his 30€ offer.

"Where are you off to next, my friend?"

"I'm going to Coral Bay," I responded enthusiastically as I definitively knew my next stop.

"I'm going to Coral Bay; you can ride with me." Chris's response was music to my ears. This would save me at least an hour of multiple bus rides and confusion before I could get there. When I asked what the cost would be, he let me know that it was nothing. He was heading in that direction anyway, and we were friends. Cypriots help out their friends and take care of each other.

As we learned earlier, making relationships in your quest to become elite is more important than making sales. It will pay you dividends in the future. You may not know when, but they will pay off. Being elite means you trust the process with no comprehension of the timeline. The timeline doesn't matter. You do the right activities, and it will all circle back in due time. Be patient and believe in the professional sales process. If you keep your activity high enough, you'll always have different activities circling back at different times.

As we drove to Coral Bay, I felt triumphant about walking away from the 30€ price that I'd now taken all the way down to free. Chris's jeep was filled with four Russians—a couple and a mom with her thirteen-year-old daughter—and a translator. Cyprus is a popular summer destination for Russians; it's a quick flight.

As I explained the story of my travels, my uncle who had lived in Nicosia, my book, and the traveling concepts of sales, it was being translated into Russian for the entire group. They were fascinated; I won over the jeep and went from a traveling freeloader to the entertainment of the ride.

We stopped at a banana farm where Chris took my picture next to a banana tree. We then went to the Sea Caves, and the young Russian girl, Oliana, had a request for a photograph with me. Chris and I laughed because I'd turned into a tourist attraction of my own. I happily took a picture with her and one with Chris, my now current client and friend.

To see pictures from the Paphos excursion and around the island, go to www.grassisbrowner.com.

In professional sales, negotiation occurs throughout your entire presentation. It's not just myself who is excited about getting a deal. Everyone wants to feel like they got an amazing deal. Therefore, part of your negotiation is telling your prospect that they're getting a great deal.

When you are willing to provide them with your personal cell phone and excellent service, they are getting a phenomenal deal regardless of the price. Conducting yourself in an elite manner allows you to become the product or service differentiator because they are unable to get your service anywhere else. You are unique and different from every other sales rep out there. Throughout your presentation, you will want to reiterate your value points and confirm that they are getting the best deal by moving forward with you and your company. When done the right way, they will believe it and understand the value that you represent.

In order for potential clients to understand your value, you need to be properly prepared for your meeting, like we discussed in chapter 4. By coming prepared, you've immediately differentiated yourself from your competition. Now it's important that you execute a professional sales meeting with yet another structured agenda.

"Just to set the agenda for our meeting. We're going to spend about forty-five minutes to an hour together depending on questions. I'll start by asking you a few questions about your business to find out your specific needs. I will then formulate my presentation based on what will be of interest to you and your company. I ask that you not worry about the price as you'll be getting a great deal. We couldn't have _____ clients unless

(Number)

our product was priced at a point that made sense. After we go through the presentation, I will walk you through everything that you'll be receiving—and the cost. Once again, you'll be getting an awesome deal, so no need to worry. (smile/laugh) As long as everything makes sense, it's really easy to get you set up so I'll be asking for your business and answering any of your questions throughout my presentation. Does that sound like a fair agenda?"

You are starting to see that being elite does not mean you need to learn and memorize a hundred different word tracks. The word track I've used to set the agenda for a current client appointment, lost client appointment, and new prospect are all very similar. Learning one of them will allow you to quickly adapt to the other two situations along with your own company, industry, and style.

Each agenda gives you a process where your presentation skills are executed the correct way and on purpose. It also provides the prospect with a comfort level that you will not be wasting their time. You've properly set their expectations. Let's jump into the presentation of your proposal now that you have a baseline on why this is the proper agenda.

If you do not have a formal preprinted proposal that you bring to your appointments, you will need to create one. Your proposal should include everything the client is getting by signing up with your product or service. You'll want to make sure that all of the value is itemized so they truly feel as if they are getting a lot for the cost. Walk them through each line item and re-explain each individual value point that is included.

Provide your highest revenue product, regardless if it is the right fit for the client.

Your proposal should also provide your highest revenue product, regardless if it is the right fit for the client. This is known as top-down selling. If you ever buy a sales book that coaches on bottom-up selling, you'll want to immediately recycle it. It's the right thing to do unless you need to use it as a fire starter. As I get into the details as to why, I am making this strong statement to sell you on the importance of top-down selling and the importance it will play in every negotiation you have.

If the highest revenue product or service does not make sense for the prospect, you will cross out the products that they don't need and reduce the price while presenting the proposal. Remember, everyone wants a great deal. Without even discounting, you will increase your credibility and trust with the client. You instantly make them feel as if they are getting a great deal when you lower their pricing. You have truly customized your presentation to their needs, and they will appreciate it.

This should also be the same practice for someone who is price sensitive and has made this clear throughout your presentation.

As you take them through the proposal, use the following word track:

"Let me just walk you through the proposal so you have a complete understanding of everything that is included. It really is a great deal to sign up with _____. We couldn't have _____
(Your Company) (Number)
clients if it wasn't an awesome deal."

Reminding them of the number of clients you have is your verification of why it is such a good deal. There is safety in numbers. If you don't have many clients signed up, let them know that this is why your company is growing so rapidly. Also, where applicable, you can say, "It is why _____ referred me to you." The most important thing to do is to provide them with a reason as to why your product or service is the best deal. The elite aren't just being persuasive, they are educating by defending their statements and explaining why.

Go through each bullet point of the products and value propositions your company offers. When you get to the price, it's important that you say "only" and, once again, "You're getting a great deal." Many times, business owners don't know what the price should be for your product or service. Save them the time of doing the research and tell them it's a great deal as you assume the sale.

> "The price is only _____. You're getting a great deal. In order to get you squared away, I just need a couple of signatures and some basic information. What is the Federal I.D. number for the business?"

As you can see in this word track, I believe in the assumptive close. If you have earned the right and done your job, the close should merely be the logical conclusion to your presentation. Roll right into doing what you need to sign up the business. If your sale does not require their Federal I.D., you'll want to substitute the last line of the word track for something you actually need in order to move forward.

You'll get one of two possible negotiation outcomes from your close:

1. They say yes and sign up with no contention on the price.

2. They say no or they need to think about it.

Let's discuss these. The first is my favorite and the easiest. While it may seem obvious, we'll go through the less obvious. As you collect their signatures and the necessary information to sign up, you need to understand that you do not have a sale yet. You only have a sale once they start paying for and using your product or service.

Revenue needs to start coming in to your company in order for it to truly be a sale. As a result, many sales representatives don't understand that they need to keep selling as they collect signatures. Confirm that they've made a great decision. If you don't, you will have a higher percentage of sales fall out compared to the elite. The elite lock in their sales and make their prospects feel excited and confident in their decision to move forward.

Use one or both of these word tracks to provide positive confirmation as you complete the sign-up process with your new client.

- "This is a great decision for your business. I'm really excited that we'll be working together."

- "My favorite part of working for _____ (Your Company) is the amazing service we provide. I'm excited for you to experience the service and I know this is the right decision for your company."

As we learned in the introduction, you should feel free to personalize the word tracks and make them your own. The concept is what will effectively increase your sales. Incorporate yourself to make sure you believe in what you are saying.

As a second level of locking in your sale, you should always send a welcome email to your client within twenty-four hours. It should be saved as an email template, so you can quickly change and personalize this information. But treat this email as your personal receipt and thank you for signing up. This thirty-second email will ensure that your sales are actually sales.

As you grow your referral army, you should take the next step in welcoming your new client to your company. Send them a personal thank you card in the mail. No one writes letters anymore, so when you get a greeting card, you remember it and the person who sent it. This is an elite practice to build your army and can be done in front of the television at night during commercials. Buy blank thank you cards in bulk and write the following along with your own personal touch:

"Dear _____ ,

I just wanted to send a personal thank you for signing up with _____. I know you'll enjoy
(Your Company)
the service we provide and please let me know if you need anything. Remember, I do rely on referrals from my current clients to stay busy, so I thank you in advance for your help. It personally means a lot to me.

Thank you again and take care,

Jon Markwardt

Personal Cell Phone: (___)____-_____"

Not only am I making the transaction personal by writing the thank you card, but I also make it explicit by using the word "personal" in the thank you card three times and providing my "personal" cell phone number again. I'm making it okay for them to call me if they need something. I know that when they do, it creates obligation for them to refer me as I over and over again win the right for their referrals.

But let's say the prospect says no or that they need to think about it.

If your prospect needs to think about it, they are effectively saying no. Treat both of these the same way. It is your job to get curious and find out why they are either saying no or need to think about it. Do they feel there is value missing from your product? Does the price not work for them? What is holding them back from moving forward today?

Elite sales representatives are direct. They strongly believe in not leaving anything as a true pending. They push hard to get a yes or no, and they celebrate them both equally. The no will eventually turn into a sale if you use strategic follow-up and earn the right.

The pending will cost you money. If your prospect does not give you a direct answer, you will spend countless hours following up via email, phone calls, and even dropping by their location. This is the worst possible result, as it will prevent you from building your pipeline elsewhere. Be direct and try the following word track:

> "When someone wants to think about it, it often means something is missing from my product or they are uncomfortable with my price. Is one of these holding you back from moving forward today?"

Like Princess 3 taught us in chapter 3, your job is to ask why. You should not leave until you get an answer. There are some situations in which someone can't move forward with you due to needing approval from a board or partner, and it is the only thing holding them back. To make sure you've done your job, use the following word track:

> "If the decision were entirely up to you, is this something you would move forward with today?"

If they say no, you can now go into the service conversation or the price conversation. If they say yes, you will confirm that they are correct in their decision-making process and find out what you can do to move things forward. As a result of not being able to get the sale today, your "sale" is to now set the follow-up appointment to take care of signatures and move things forward at a later date.

If they aren't willing to set the follow-up appointment, the reality is that there is something holding them back. Stay curious and find out what is preventing them from setting the follow-up appointment to move things forward.

Product or Service Conversation

These are my favorite conversations because I represent a great product. If I've missed something that was important to them, it now becomes my top priority to reengage the client and transform them into an excited and raving fan of my product as I sign them up. Your entire conversation needs to focus on what truly is important to their business that was not discovered in the meeting.

As an elite sales representative, you know the product better than anyone else. And clients that stump you are helping you grow your knowledge. Do not wait to get them their answer. And do not guess. This is not a game. This is their business, and you are not allowed to mess with their business.

I am protective over buyers because poor salespeople give the profession a bad name. Make sure you separate yourself from these individuals. You must be seen as someone they trust as a consultant, not just a sales representative trying to sell them something. When you don't know something, be direct.

"Wow. That's a great question. I actually don't know the answer to that. I have an idea, but I never guess. It's not how I do business. I'm going to call our service department on speaker phone. Not only will we get your answer, but you'll see how great and quick our service is."

Please note that you will need to have a supportive service department you can call in order to use this as your response. If you do not and have no way of getting the answer immediately through a manager or a peer, you are now forced into a situation where you've essentially created your own pending. It's why elite sales representatives know the product and service better than anyone else. Pendings are not good for your efficiency.

Failing

Having a prospect stump you is a great thing. I absolutely love failing. No, I'm not crazy; I realize this is now the second time we're covering failing, but I'm doing this to stress the importance. Failing makes you learn. I've failed as much as anyone in sales, and I got better as I continually learned from my mistakes. It's important to understand that everyone fails. And we all fail on more than one occasion.

However, there is no better way to remember the right way to do something than failing miserably. You'll never forget. When a prospect stumps you during a presentation, you will learn that answer for all future prospects. One of the best ways to grow your knowledge is one failure at a time.

The best negotiation I've experienced thus far in Cyprus happened after I got sick of waiting for the bus. I'd been walking by a place that rents scooters every day on the way to my office café. And every day, I'd been talking to Ival, who later became one of my friends in Cyprus. He is what I would call a "car salesman." He does not do professional sales in the slightest, but he is no novice to negotiation.

Ival said the standard price for a scooter for one day was 20€ ($24 US). If I rented it for two weeks or longer, Ival would drop the price to 10€ ($12 US) per day. I wanted to rent a scooter for thirty days to truly explore the island and leave the bus behind me. The pain of the bus was starting to diminish my negotiation skills, but I was determined to follow my normal process.

I wanted to get him down to 200€ ($240 US) for the entire month. He made a great point about the luxury of renting: if I had any problems, I was able to call a number and they'd come pick up me along with the bike. This is how he handled my objection of trying to find a used one online, then just selling it before I leave the island. I was impressed and soon-to-be sold.

Ival offered me the scooter for thirty days at 280€ ($335 US). This was his cheapest offer, but I still walked away. The next day, we were back to 300€ ($360 US). He told me that I'd missed out on 280€. He explained that with the insurance they provided, it didn't make sense to rent it for less than 10€ a day. I walked away again and went back to my wonderful bus system.

A few days later, Ival had a surplus of scooters. He normally didn't have that many, and I could tell this was the time to negotiate. Also, the night before, I'd waited for the bus for half an hour. When the bus finally arrived, it was too full for me to get on. I walked back to my apartment, and the pain of not renting a scooter was at an all-time high.

Ival's value proposition was getting stronger by the day.

The Negotiation Battle

With his surplus of scooters, I offered Ival 250€ ($300 US) for the thirty days. He said that he would do it, but only if I did it right now and he would never offer me this deal again. He did such a great job of creating the urgency that I immediately agree to the deal. I had my new transportation, and I was satisfied with my negotiation. Although I felt Ival won the negotiation battle, I was happy to be done with the bus.

The next day I drove around the island to the point where I got lost. Getting lost is the best way for me to intentionally fail and learn my way around. But there was no better experience of failure than when I started to contemplate stopping to ask for directions. As I took a left down an unfamiliar street, I was no longer thinking about driving. All I was thinking about was trying to figure out where I was and how to get back to my apartment.

I let my natural instincts do the driving. As I turned a curve in the road, I was looking straight at a taxi driver coming at me. I immediately adjusted my scooter back to the left side of the road and thus I avoided a quick end to my book and travels.

"Left Side of the Road. Never Forget!"

Price Conversation

Ival gave us a perfect example of how to set the bar and how to be willing to walk away. While I was playing the same game, no one would have ever won if Ival wasn't willing to bend on his price a little to get the sale. In turn, I needed to do the same.

Effectively presenting your proposal with your highest revenue product sets the bar where it needs to be for a healthy negotiation. If you have the ability to charge a set-up, this should always be marked in full. And it should never be immediately waived. You want to have as many chips as possible to play with in your negotiation.

As the negotiation starts, you are looking to establish one fact. At what price will they move forward with your product or service today? Obviously, we want that price to be as high as possible. But remember, your prospect is looking to feel good about the deal they are receiving and is most likely skilled at negotiating as well. Business owners negotiate for multiple products and services. You are not their first negotiation, and successful business owners are adept negotiators.

The best place to start is to reiterate your value and let them know that, in the business world, you get what you pay for. You have an exceptional product and that's why your price is what it is. Let them know you are proud of your price. If all they are looking for is the cheapest product, you are not the right company for their business. This will lay the groundwork on the negotiation if they are not willing to move forward at your current price. As you've already set the bar, you can now put it in their court.

> "This being said, I do have a little wiggle room in my pricing. What would it take for you to move forward today?"

You will find that as you reiterate the value, the discount that they respond with is far less than you think would be required. If you've done a great job selling, they are looking to buy and just want to make sure they are getting a good deal. Despite the lower price, Ival was still happy with the sale of the scooter. And I felt obligated to buy from him rather than from someone else since we'd been talking every day and developed a friendship.

Once the prospect names the price, the negotiation continues from there. You can either continue the negotiation with a price somewhere in the middle, or you can accept their terms if the pricing is still good revenue for you and your company. Regardless of how you pursue the negotiation, I always require referrals when I provide a discount.

> "Since I'm providing you with a discount to sign up, I need your help with a referral. But because I'm giving you such a great deal, I would really appreciate if you didn't tell them the discount that I've given you. I'm not allowed to offer that deal to everyone I sign up."

This statement makes them feel special and as if they've received a satisfying deal. It also makes them feel obligated to refer you. And once again, it is all true. If you are in sales, I'm sure you know of "another" sales representative who has a discounting problem. Eventually, this will lead to what I call "discount probation." Discount probation is when the representative discounts too great and too often that they are no longer allowed to sell anything with a discount until they can be retrained on selling the value of the product or service.

The other way to negotiate allows you to take complete control of the negotiation as you hold your ground based on your sales instincts. Most of the time, you are able to feel out how much of a discount they will need to move forward. You may even know what they are paying for their current product or service. At this point, you will give them a discount that you feel comfortable with and let them know that it is your maximum discount.

"As a result of _____ (Reason), I am able to provide you with a _____ percent discount. This is the best price that I can offer you. If it needs to be one penny cheaper, I'm unable to do business with you. You really are getting a great deal to sign up."

Here are examples of reasons you may use:

1. They were referred by _____.
2. They are a lost client.
3. It is the end of the month, quarter, or year.

Say the Percentage

Typically, you will want to say the percentage of the discount unless you have a high revenue product. You're looking to use whichever one sounds bigger. You may even want to annualize the savings based on your conversation.

Remember, people want to hear they're getting a deal. Knowing that you can't give them the price one penny cheaper makes your prospect feel good about the deal. Once again, this statement needs to be true. It's why there should be additional layers in your company in order to discount. The sales representative should have a threshold they can go to. They should then have an additional threshold with approval by a manager. And there should be a final threshold for an approval by a regional or VP. This allows your statement to be honest with whatever you choose based on the situation.

For example, you may be allowed to do a 10 percent discount on your own, a 20 percent discount with manager approval, and a 25 percent discount with VP approval. In each scenario, you are unable to go to the next level without additional approvals, so your original statement can start at 10 percent. If it needs to go higher, you can respond:

> "I really can't go any higher than a 10 percent discount. The only way this has ever been done before is by getting my manager involved. But I can tell you it has been done before. I will go to bat for you and get the 15 percent discount taken care of as long as we can take care of the paperwork today. It only takes five minutes to get you set up. Do you have a voided check so we can move forward?"

I go straight back to my assumptive sale. I am in the driver's seat. I am negotiating to get the highest revenue I can for myself and my company. Most importantly, I am doing so with complete honesty as I am straightforward throughout the entire process. The result is the prospect feeling confident and excited about their transaction and my credibility is maintained throughout the entire process.

The discount thresholds provide the prospect with the knowledge that I am willing to walk away. It shares that they are at a maximum discount. This gives me leverage to close for the deal and establish whether or not they are interested in buying. While it's important for the prospect to understand that you're willing to walk away, it's equally crucial to make sure the prospect feels important. Throughout the presentation, make sure you are letting the prospect know how much you'd like to be doing business with them and that they would really benefit from your product or service.

Get Referrals

You are worth full price. You are different than all the other sales representatives out there watching TV and sleeping in. Believe in yourself and your product.

Even if you discounted your product, you are the best restaurant in town, and your new client should be referring you to all their friends and family. Believe it like the sky is blue and collect on your hard work. You earned the right and you should now have an additional soldier in your referral army.

As we look back at what we've learned in this chapter on negotiation, please understand that negotiation is an art. You will get better at it as you develop your negotiation skills over time. Negotiation is something that is most effectively learned through failure. As you fail, get the unit over the revenue. Sign up the client and learn when you could have gotten them with a lower discount or no discount at all. Self-evaluate and lean on your mentors and coaches for practices on taking your negotiation skills to the next level. Your two questions after each presentation should be:

1. What did I do well?

2. What can I do better?

Each company has a different policy on discounting. You'll want to apply whatever your policy is to the concepts in this chapter. If you are unable to provide any type of discount, you are in a great situation. You most likely represent an extremely high quality product or service. Sell the value of the product and hold your ground. You'll be able to be straightforward and honest with the situation that all clients pay the same price for your product or service because it is a great deal, and this is why your company is not open to negotiation.

No one is perfect, so don't worry about negotiating every sale to your maximum revenue. At some point, everyone drives on the wrong side of the road. Celebrate your successes and celebrate your failures. As long as you don't drive into a taxi head on, you are learning and you are growing. Remember, if you're not getting better, you're dead. Just make sure you swerve fast enough to the left side of the road—or is it the right?

11

The Sales Science Experiment

Negotiation taught us how to effectively generate your sale with the largest revenue possible. However, the most crucial part of your negotiation will always fall on your ability to handle objections. Handling objections is extremely critical to having success during the negotiation process.

Objections are very much individualized across industries, companies, services, and products. As a result, this chapter requires the most written work in understanding the objections you are likely to face and how to effectively handle them at your company. Please make sure you have a pen or pencil as we navigate through this chapter together. Remember, you are looking to expand your sales skills and become elite. The exercises throughout the book and specifically in this chapter will help you do so.

As I have booked out my travel, I have been exclusively staying in vacation rentals found through online sites. I enjoy the comforts of living in a fully furnished home or apartment as opposed to a hotel. It's also much easier to negotiate with a homeowner as opposed to a hotel. And I do enjoy the art of each negotiation whether I am buying or selling. Some people are passionate about surfing. I am passionate about sales and negotiation.

I was traveling in Cyprus during high season, so there were a lot of tourists on the island who drive the prices up. Most of the one-bedroom places on these websites are a minimum of $100 per night with many places over $200 per night that have somewhat similar accommodations. While I was not willing to compromise on the luxury of the home, I was also not willing to pay $100 per night or more.

Because I was traveling for an extended period, I preferred to not be spending $3,000 or more per month on my housing. At $3,000 per month, it would make me feel as if I should buy a time-share. While I don't believe in the value received through owning a time-share, I love listening to time-share presentations. I find time-share sales reps to always represent their *attitude* as *awesome* as they check two of the As with every presentation I attend.

I was once in Las Vegas for a time-share presentation that I will never forget. You would have thought Bill was on some type of drug as he excitedly ran around the room high-fiving everyone. He stopped to address everyone's biggest objection in the room that they were not looking to buy. "Guys, all I'm asking is that you keep an open mind. The mind is the same as a parachute. When it's open, all is good. When it's closed, you're in trouble."

While I don't have a chapter about running around and high-fiving everyone, I'll still high-five anyone with an awesome attitude. Bill had my attention as he rattled off a comical and semi-effective sales pitch for the room. But as for me, I still don't own a time-share. So I had some work to do on my own to secure my stays at reasonable rates.

If you search for something low priced in the areas where I was staying on the east side of the island, you will find a couple of places where you "share" a home, are far from the sea, or are not accommodated with the luxuries that make home travel preferable over hotel travel. As a result, this meant that I needed to walk away from a number of different properties that didn't fit my needs and suitable properties that weren't willing to lower their price. I also had to get really good at handling my biggest objection: "It's high season. Please look around. All of the costs are up."

Do you know your biggest objections? Do you know the best way to handle them? Do you continually evaluate these objections, your responses, and your results? Take time to jot down your three biggest objections to someone signing up for your company.

Biggest Objections:
1. _____
2. _____
3. _____

Immediately Respond with Your Value Proposition

I handled my biggest objection by connecting with the homeowner. My first value proposition is this: "I completely understand. I own a home in San Diego, California, and have it rented out during my travels." It is important to understand their concern and not skip over it. But you'll need to address it.

I go on to explain that the amount of rent I receive is only half of my concern when I rent my property. As a result of understanding home ownership, I will be very respectful of their home. I'm able to take it a step further as I know I'm a much better tenant than some of their other inquiries. I express that there is inherent value to having a single, traveling author stay in their home as opposed to a bunch of twenty-one-year-olds on holiday from London.

The Sales Laboratory

Sales is one gigantic science experiment. In this scenario, the constant is the consistent objection you hear. The variable will be the value proposition you respond with for that objection. By continuing to experiment with your variable, you are able to optimize the results of your science experiment.

Knowing your product or service doesn't mean you just know a long list of value propositions for what you do. It also means that you know what you don't do and what the most common objections are for not signing up with your product or service. Honing your craft allows you to customize and find the best ways to handle these objections.

Successful people utilize other successful people, concepts, and ideas to stretch the boundaries of success.

Likewise, this is why it is intrinsically important that you surround yourself with other top representatives of your company. They are performing the exact same science experiment on a daily basis and can provide you with more data than you will be able to gather on your own. There is no reason for you to reinvent the wheel.

The swimsuit was invented in the eighteenth century, but it wasn't until 1946 that the bikini was born. Louis Réard invented the bikini by expanding and customizing an entire line of clothing that was already popular. Swimwear entered into a new era as Réard altered this line of clothing to an entirely new and popular product. Successful people utilize other successful people, concepts, and ideas to stretch the boundaries of success. Surround yourself with successful people as you stretch best sales practices into the next bikini.

Take a moment to respond to your three biggest objections here. Write down your responses. Please remember, your answers are variables. You should constantly be evaluating and upgrading your variables. These are pencil answers as opposed to pen. Take the exercise a step further and reach out to top representatives at your company to see how they respond to the objections you itemized earlier.

Hint: Each response should provide a value proposition to support moving forward with your product or service as you handle the objection.

Response to Objections:

1. _____
2. _____
3. _____

Pain

There is always a certain amount of pain for not signing up with a quality product or service. You may be required to navigate yourself to the other side of the island on your own without a guided tour. Maybe you are forced to do additional work for your business on your own rather than outsource it. Or, worse, maybe you have six young adults trashing your summer home when they said there were only four coming.

Telling a detailed story of the pain provides an explanation of the value your product or service will represent. This is often a positive way to handle the objection. Stories sell. And in many cases the pain is worth the additional cost. Most people will pay for comfort over simply shopping on price.

If it is strictly a price-based decision, pain is often a way to figure out that it's not just about price. No one wants the painful result. Who would ever want their home trashed by a bunch of kids on a holiday weekend? As a result, you will steer your conversation away from pricing and back to the value you represent. Elite sales representatives sell on value, not on price.

Read and practice this power statement.

> "I sell on value, not on price."

Understanding the intrinsic value of your product means you are able to illustrate the pain the prospect will receive when they don't sign up with you. This is not an opportunity to be threatening. It's an opportunity to tell a story.

Elite sales representatives are genuinely concerned about their prospects. Their number-one objective is to earn the right. As they look to earn the right, they are attempting to protect their prospect's business. Protecting their business should include utilizing your product or service for the benefits it will provide them and their company.

Please take a moment to write down three areas of pain your prospect could encounter if they don't move forward with your product or service. Make it your mission to continually collect stories and testimonial letters on these specific pain points to handle objections moving forward. If you do not currently have any stories, you will need to reach out to your manager and peers for their stories that you can use in your presentation until you have your own.

Pain Points:

1. _____
2. _____
3. _____

Keep in mind, most stories in B2B sales deal with failing to outsource; something doesn't get done correctly that causes pain, or the owner's time is spent on a non-revenue generating activity. A decision by the prospect to not outsource their website design could result in countless hours fumbling through the project only to finish with a less than desirable result.

Help

It's my favorite four-letter word: *help*. As a result of being a traveling author, I was traveling on limited funds. I had no source of income, so as a result I was price conscious.

I continue to ask you, the reader, to refer your friends and family to this book and help it become a best seller. However, the creation process of this book did not generate any income. In fact, I spent funds to produce this book that were all expenses to build a quality product I believe in.

As my accountant said, you do not have a business until you start generating income. During the writing of the book, I had a hobby. Many people want to be helpful because it feels great to do things for other people, but they also help themselves, for example, by getting a great tenant in their vacation rental.

There are multiple ways that you can ask for help during your professional objection handling. The most common way is by dealing with the price objection. When price is a concern, you can steer them to your current client program. Be direct in your approach by saying that by referring you, you can help them on the cost, and it really helps you as well.

If their price objection requires you to provide them with a discount to win their business, you should make sure to ask for a favor in return—a referral. But more importantly, you'll want to get their help in coming to a price that they are willing to move forward on today. The goal is to add to your referral army or get a solid no and understand why. Everyone has a maximum discount, and if they aren't willing to help you by staying within a reasonable price to sign up, they can help you at a later date as you add them to your CRM tool for strategic follow-up.

Be direct on the exact help that you are looking for. You wouldn't want a taxi showing up to your burning building instead of a fire truck. Your job is to find great businesses and sign them up for your awesome service. Let them know that you think they would benefit from your product or service, and it really helps your company to have quality businesses, like theirs, as current clients.

Establish a Personal Connection of Trust and Longevity

All of my stays involved written and verbal communication prior to the transaction. Establishing the rapport and validity of my respect and care for their home provided intrinsic value that had homeowners choosing me at a lower cost compared to other inquiries.

I never stayed fewer than seven nights on my travels, so making more per night on a shorter stay ended up being less than my longer stays at each location. Furthermore, there was the opportunity for me to come back since each location knew I was staying in Cyprus into September. This happened with the apartment I stayed at in Protaras.

"Ask for help like your building is on fire."

The owner, Joyce, was from Ireland and really identified with my story; she appreciated my respect to her and her home. While I left at the end of July, I moved back the second half of August. Once again, I negotiated a much lower price than the advertised rate.

Once I established my credibility of doing business with each one of these locations, I opened the door to return at a lower than advertised price. Kyriakos, from my Limassol studio, touched a special place in my heart when he asked that I refer my friends and family to his location. Since Kyriakos earned the right and asked for the referral, I will happily refer any friends or family to his studio if they should travel to Limassol.

Close the Business

Life is less expensive for those who are able to negotiate at an elite level. Not only will you make more money, but your costs go down substantially. As a result of renting out my own home in San Diego and negotiating the rates for my stays in Cyprus, I was able to live in Cyprus and write this book for a net cost of less than $50 *per month* for my housing expenses as I traveled. This afforded me the ability to not deal with the economic stress that is normally incurred through extended travel.

Please understand that the entire world is negotiable. When you are able to handle objections quickly and negotiate the right way, you are able to maximize your revenue or minimize your cost in the negotiation. However, the average person in today's society does not take advantage of this fact or know how to do so. Negotiation is a skill that many people lack and have no interest in acquiring. However, acquiring negotiation and objection-handling skills will change your life both inside and outside your professional work.

You Must Handle All Unspoken Objections

The reason I have had luxurious travel at half the rate is that, during my negotiations, I became adept at handling my number-one objection, which was that the going rate is much higher than what I was offering to pay. I addressed this objection whether it was spoken or not. I understood the real value of renting to me was the fear of not renting out their place to anyone when they could have had me at the lower rate.

There was also an unspoken objection that I may not really be who I say I am. Maybe I'm just like my previous example. It's possible that I could be four young adults that in actuality are six fraternity boys destroying the place for an entire week and disturbing every neighbor on the block. As a result, my ability to handle my objections only went as far as my ability to establish my credibility.

Vacation rental websites typically allow you to create your own profile, add a picture, and write a description. My profiles were fully built out describing who I am and what I was doing on my travels. My picture was the same one I was using for LinkedIn: professionally taken, sporting a suit. I used my first and last name in all email correspondence to provide confidence if they would like to Google me or connect to me on any of my social networks.

I knew some people may question whether I truly was a single, traveling author; therefore, I needed to handle this objection. It was just one more unspoken objection that

I wanted to get ahead of. The time-share salesman, Bill, illustrated this concept perfectly as I later learned his quote about the parachute was somewhat commonly used in time-share presentations.

If you are a small company that is growing, the prospect has most likely never heard of you. While they may not directly tell you they've never heard of you, you will need to explain why you are not as well-known as the bigger companies. Be direct. Address the unspoken objections and be two steps ahead of your prospect to gain your credibility and establish their comfort with you and your product or service.

> "The number-one reason why you may not have heard about my company is we are new and growing at a rapid rate. The best time to get involved with us is now, so you can take advantage of our current offers. I wouldn't be working for this company if I didn't believe in what we're doing, and I'd love the opportunity to show your business why we are attracting so many new clients."

Take some time to write down your unspoken objections.

1. _____
2. _____
3. _____

Grow your Knowledge and Credibility

As you become the expert of your craft, you will find that you can handle just about every question or objection. As a result, you'll start to enjoy objections. Your prospect will navigate your pitch to exactly what matters to them as they perform your needs analysis for you and help you customize your presentation for them.

Your response will become almost robotic as objections are fired at you. It is important that you quickly respond with confidence. And the most important part of handling your objections is to say something. Whether you have the perfect answer or not, you'll need to be able to readily defend your product. Here's your new word track for handling objections:

> "That actually makes you a perfect fit for _____ (Your Company). One of the primary reasons so many businesses have signed up for our product is _____." (Value Proposition)

Let's play this one out as a business banker with the objection being the hassle of switching your business bank account:

"That actually makes you a perfect fit for The Bank of Awesome. The number-one reason so many businesses have signed up for our bank is we assist you with the entire transition. I can even provide you with testimonial letters from clients who have taken time out of their day to write about how smooth the transition was for their company."

The first part of handling this objection with the word track is crucial to your response oozing confidence. I call it a transitionary statement. No matter what the objection is, you can always respond with the first two sentences of this word track. As you commit those first two sentences to permanent memory and rattle them off, it gives you time to think about what value statement you want to respond with as you quickly handle their objection.

As I conclude this chapter on handling objections, commit yourself to continually getting better. If you believe you have the best response for all of your objections, you most certainly do not. Part of being elite is committing to the research of upgrading your variables. The art of objection handling goes hand-in-hand with the art of negotiation. Becoming elite in both affords you opportunities that others don't have. Besides, how else would I be able to stay on an exotic Mediterranean island for less than $50 a month?

12

You Are Legend

Now that we've learned about negotiation and handling objections, it's time you understand where one of your biggest negotiations should be taking place. Surprisingly, most sales representatives never realize it. Your internal negotiations within your company and with your manager become vital to not only yourself but to your entire sales organization.

In the business format, it is a common belief that the top 1 percent of your company's sales organization will assume a leadership role. Much has been given to them and often more is expected from them by the executive team. These sales leaders have an opportunity to provide intrinsic feedback to the executives and the company. Done with knowledge and the right intention, such feedback will produce a positive effect on the lives of each person in the sales organization and strengthen the company as a whole.

However too often these elite representatives only watch out for themselves. While it is not your company's job to proactively give you a raise, expand your territory, or provide you with additional resources, this seems to be the overwhelming cry of top representatives to expand on what they have worked for. The reality is when you provide intrinsic value to the organization beyond your sales skills, smart organizations will always take care of their top talent; they have to for the greater benefit of the company.

For those of you who achieve the recognition and success of becoming the top 1 percent of your entire sales organization, I encourage you to think differently. Concentrate your requests and efforts with management and the executive team to push on the quality of the product. Push toward providing better service for your customers. Provide feedback on better internal processes. And put yourself in a position to test out new products and processes in order to trail blaze change for the company and the sales organization.

As a result of using your achievements for the greater good, you will open up your career path to a world of numerous opportunities.

For those of you who are still growing your green grass, you need to understand how to utilize your direct manager to assist you on landscaping your yard. Not only is your manager incentivized to help you become successful, it's their job. Put them to work to create more income for both of you.

The reason this concept of managing your manager even exists is because many sales managers do not understand how to assist their team in taking their skills to the next level. The reality is elite sales professionals rarely make elite sales leaders. Most of the time elite sales representatives aren't even interested in pursuing a career in sales management.

As a result, your growth into an elite sales professional may not always have the assistance of a coach that has been there before. This chapter serves as a reminder that your sales manager is still on your same team. It is vital to have an open line of communication with your manager, so they know how to hold you accountable and assist in pushing your activity to water your green grass.

"Manage Your Manager."

As a child, you enjoyed managing your manager (parents) on your birthday. And you were really good at it. As we get older, we often shy away from the directness that we had in our childhood. A healthy relationship with your manager is all about communication, not demands. It is important you provide your manager with respect and at the same time ask for assistance where you need it in your quest to become elite.

I am not one for birthdays, but the year I was in Cyprus, I celebrated my birthday there. On a day that I may shy away from, I was thrilled not to have any managers (friends or family) in my life on this island that required me to do anything. I was excited to have a frappe with my friends at my office café and a whiskey with my scooter salesman, Ival. I was able to add in some light reading on the beach and some swimming in the sea to provide myself with a day that was equivalent to a ten-year-old spending their birthday at Disneyland.

For me, I was excited for a birthday where I didn't have friends forcing me to go out for dinner or drinks. I didn't want to manage the events of an evening. I was excited to have a casual day with my new friends in Cyprus. As I received some really nice text messages, emails, and Facebook greetings throughout the day, my biggest obligation was to simply reply "thank you" and manage my own day.

Sales managers are not mind readers.

However, being elite does not happen just once a year. The first and biggest mistake a sales representative will ever make with their manager is not getting what they need from them. Sales managers are not mind readers. They don't know what they don't know. If you don't tell them you need additional coaching, want to see your statistics at a greater frequency, or need technical training, you are once again relying on the hope strategy.

Hope is not for the elite. There is nothing better for a sales manager than to know exactly what their sales rep needs. As a result, every one-on-one I've ever conducted concludes with the following question: "What do you need from me?"

At this point, I've transferred the obligation on my sales representative to let me know what they need. And as any dedicated sales manager, I'm adaptable and there to help. All sales representatives are different, and as a result each will need something different from their manager. While the goal is for my team meetings to benefit the masses, the individual training needs to be exactly that—individual.

Whether your manager is asking you what you need or not, be direct. Close your manager on giving you what you need. You will be more successful as a result.

It is your job to give your manager the opportunity to better your career. Don't worry about anyone else's thoughts or feelings on your manager. Sell your manager on providing you with what you need to be successful. Part of how you'll do this is by developing your relationship with your manager as an internal relationship. The relationship you have with your manager also requires your own cliff-jumping experience. If your manager is not inviting you for a shared experience, you should invite them and grow the relationship.

I believe my first sales manager truly bought into me after I took him to a San Diego Padres game and bought him beers. While I was earning the right through my success within the company, I was still relatively new. At the game, we were able to get to know each other on a new level and have our cliff-jumping experience.

I was able to share my career aspirations and ask for his support along the way. From that point on, I noticed a new level of obligation that my manager had with sharing in my success and the advancement of my career. My manager was already a fan of me, but it felt as if our relationship was taken to the next level after our shared experience.

This manager continually told me how awesome I was and how grateful he was to have me on his team. This positive reinforcement not only gave me comfort in our relationship and my status within the company, but it allowed me to understand my worth to him and the team. If you are not receiving positive reinforcement from your manager, you either need to improve your performance or share a cliff-jumping experience together.

In Cyprus, I turned to my office café for my positive reinforcement from my current client, Michalis. Michalis was one of the happiest people I met on the island. He was always smiling, encouraging me on my writing, my Greek, and my various adventures. Whether I was attempting to speak Greek or telling him about my previous day's adventure, Michalis often responded with, "You are legend."

As Michalis said these three words, he motivated me to continue to write, explore, speak Greek, and share my stories with him as my friend. While you may not know where you stand with your current manager, I knew where I stood with both my professional sales manager and Michalis. I'd not only earned the right to be in their good graces, but I'd earned the right for them to become one of my biggest fans. The relationship you are striving for as you continue to grow your connection to your manager is just as Michalis told me each day at my office café.

"You are legend."

Throughout my career, I've also had managers who didn't provide me with positive reinforcement. In fact, they may have had a much different saying about me. While the opposite relationship is not the desirable one, it does occur. And should you repeatedly attempt to close your manager on providing you with something you need to be successful to no avail, you will need to be direct again. You are in sales. Be proud of what you do. Sell your manager on providing you with what you need.

It's an age-old saying, but, "The squeaky wheel gets the grease." You will produce more with your manager contributing to your success. So it becomes your job to negotiate this happening internally to grow your green grass.

When your manager is helping you and your business grow, you need to make sure your manager knows that they are legend. Managers need your appreciation and recognition as much as you need it from them. Positive reinforcement to your manager will only strengthen their determination to assist your growth within the company. Great partnerships go both ways, and working together will create an opportunity for you both to achieve more as a team, as opposed to striking out on your own.

First and foremost, you need to manage your manager as a resource to operate more efficiently. They will be able to provide a large contribution in your quest to become elite. Ignoring what your manager can do for you is a mistake that will not only cost you efficiency, but will also cost you production.

At the same time, it is wise to understand that you will become elite through your own merit. No manager or leader can ever make you elite. You will achieve this status on your own. It is more important that you believe in yourself as opposed to having Michalis cheer you on each day.

Internal Rewards of Becoming Elite

Being elite often means you will be given additional benefits within your company. As a result of selling more, you will make more money and receive recognition. But you may also have the opportunity to increase your territory, salary, vacation time, or expense account.

You have worked hard to water your grass, and having the greenest grass on the block is something that you should enjoy. You committed to your one thousand and one activities that made you better and brought you more sales. However, gaining additional yard to water is not an opportunity to brag or gloat. This will cause problems for you with your peers and management on your company island. Islands are small, and as a result these problems may take a long time to go away. You should be gracious and flattered when you expand your territory and understand the obligation to produce more for yourself, your manager, and your company.

It is important to note again that being elite does not give you the right to abuse your newfound status. The result of this will inevitably lead to starting out with an entirely new lawn whether it be a company decision or your own.

In your expanded territory, you will need to implement the activities you initially had in your original territory and grow the business the right way. As you built things the right way in your original geography, you are able to enjoy the rewards of your referral army as you concentrate the heavy lifting on your new territory growth. Your activity and attitude in your new territory will drive how awesome your expansion will be.

Once again, these benefits come with great responsibility. While you may feel as if you've earned it, you are being given these advantages to provide greater growth to the company on a higher level than simply the sales you are producing. Take the opportunity to provide feedback seriously and concentrate on one question when given the opportunity to discuss the sales organization with the executives of your company.

"If you owned the entire company, what would you do to increase sales?"

This chapter highlights the importance of the relationship you have with your manager and company. As a reminder, it is vital that your manager is providing you with the coaching and instruction you need to perform at an elite level. Make sure you are communicating those needs to close your manager on providing you with the "birthday" that you are looking for.

The reality is that most often we do not effectively use the resources right in front of us. Your manager is not only a resource, but they are a resource that is incentivized to aid in your success. Prior to moving to the next chapter, please list the top three things you need from your manager to become elite that you are not getting today. Hold yourself accountable by bookmarking this page and discussing them with your manager in your next one-on-one.

What do I need from my manager?

1. _____

2. _____

3. _____

13

The Ice Cream Man

As I sat in my office café, I smiled after my friend Michalis walked over to excitedly greet me. It was always heartening to get a pep talk from my informal "manager" before starting my writing for the day. We chatted for a while until he asked me if I wanted my normal order.

My grass was feeling particularly green that morning; I felt as if I'd really established myself as I continued to enjoy my "normal order" each day. What I didn't realize at the time was that I'd also branded myself as the American author who came to the café every morning. Cypriots are very welcoming to everyone, and they are also curious when new people are consistently around. In a conversation with Michalis that I didn't know anyone else was paying attention to, a Cypriot gentleman and his wife became very intrigued about me and my story.

As usual, I enjoyed my time writing, along with the beautiful view. I stood up to throw the plastic glass away that no longer contained my morning beverage and walked back from the trash can. Demetrios stopped me and introduced himself and his wife, Maria. He was a pilot, well-traveled, educated, and curious to know more about me. After discussing what I was doing there and my story, we were both surprised that he knew of the previous companies I'd worked for with many of his travels to America.

"It's a small world" applied to our introduction at this remote café in Cyprus. As he took a particular interest and formed a connection with me, he asked me if he could buy me lunch. He was a very interesting guy, and I was curious about what he would like to discuss. I accepted his invitation.

We met at the restaurant next door, and we both had moussaka and a Keo. Keo is the locally brewed beer—my favorite beer on the island, and moussaka is a local dish. It's slow cooked and layered like lasagna without the pasta. It has layers of meat, potatoes, and vegetables.

As we enjoyed our meals and got to know each other better, Demetrios told me all about Cyprus and the history of the country. He went on to articulate the many benefits that businesses receive in Cyprus. He was an affluent man who had wisely invested in many properties along with being a local business owner in the capital, Nicosia.

He was at a point in his career where he was interested in doing something far more entrepreneurial. He had a lot of questions about business in the United States and ideas for himself as he searched for a possible business investment to enjoy and contribute to at this new stage in his career. I now understood why he wanted to buy me lunch.

Consistency

As I'd branded myself each day in the café as a businessman from America writing a book, Demetrios decided that it would be advantageous to get to know me over the course of a meal. We were having our cliff-jumping experience over moussaka and a Keo. I won't get into all the particulars on his entrepreneurial ideas; those were part of our private conversation. But as we got to know each other better, it became clear that he was interested in the prospect of doing business with me. I was flattered and enjoyed discussing a few of his future business ideas.

Branding myself in the café resulted in an opportunity to talk about prospective business opportunities with a new friend. When you show up every day with your "I am" statement, you will start to have other people believe it too. This is particularly relevant to how referrals work. There is a compounding equation that occurs when you practice your "I am" statement and show up each day.

I started to see this equation unfold as my inner network around Cyprus began to refer me to influential people around the island with different opportunities that would be beneficial for my book and growing my network.

During my travels and expansion of my network in Cyprus, the island became more than a place to write the book. It also became a place that I would now be targeting for sales. The book had transformed into sharing so many Cyprus stories that it only made sense to have it sold where it was written. My inner network on the island was sharing my story for me because they believed I was an American author as much as they believed the sky was blue. The results yielded opportunities that I had not initially realized.

As you've started to see how the elite handle their objections and negotiate, it is more to do with what they bring to the table over the company. They are selling the value of themselves. As a result, marketing yourself is your brand. Not your company. It is important that you brand yourself in your territory, above and beyond your company's name.

The first step in successfully branding yourself is showing up every day and doing the best job you can. The more you become involved and brand yourself in your territory, the more you will start to see that "it's a small territory."

Your current clients begin to know your lost clients who know your networking partners and eventually the place where you get your morning coffee. You become the answer to questions about your industry and are the solution for these questions as people talk about your industry in your territory. Eventually, each new business that enters your territory only has one logical person to sign up with as your referral army does the work for you.

"Protect and Serve Referrals."

Invest in Yourself

As you brand yourself in your territory, it's important that you make the investment to have everyone in your territory think about you and associate you with your industry and your company. Investing in yourself will be the greatest investment you will ever make. While early on I talked about dressing the part, I take it a step further in this chapter to talk about marketing materials that will increase awareness that all consumers and businesses need to be signing up with you and not your company.

Some of these items may be an opportunity to sell your manager on paying for the marketing materials to brand yourself. However, it's important to note that if you can't close your manager, you should believe enough in yourself to pay for these materials on your own.

> **There is no greater investment than investing in yourself.**

Postcards

Postcards have the highest ROI over any other investment that I have ever made. A small and personal note on a postcard from a place where I am on vacation is a cliff-jumping experience that creates obligation for under a dollar. I believe they have the highest ROI compared to any marketing I've ever done because they are always genuine. I sincerely thought of my client or networking partner while I was on my vacation and took the time to let them know.

Your competition does not send postcards. They lie around at the pool, they sit by the sea, and they only worry about fixing their farmer's tan. I have sent twenty-five postcards so far on my trip. Many are to family and friends, but I also sent postcards to the law firm that trademarked the title of this book, the accounting firm that advised me on this business venture, and people I planned to work with when I moved back to my home in California.

All of the postcards have been genuine, yet some of them provided professional benefits as well. Imagine the additional obligation created as you are building a referral relationship in your territory.

The other nice thing about postcards is, when you are elite, you are able to think outside the box and operate more efficiently. I'm not asking that you drive your wife or husband crazy as you write out twenty-five postcards by the pool. We are in an ecommerce society where you don't have to be in the location to purchase your postcards.

As a result, you can purchase the postcards prior to your trip from many online venues that sell them from some of the more touristy cities you may be visiting. When this option isn't available, you can usually call your hotel or work it out with the person you are renting your vacation home from to purchase and mail you a group of postcards prior to even leaving the comfort of your own home. As a result, you'll be able to write your notes and address your postcards on the plane while other people are watching a movie or reading a gossip magazine. Purchase the stamps and mail when you are in your location during the first few days of your holiday and enjoy your vacation.

There is no better branding than something hanging up in someone's office that reminds them of you each day. For under a dollar, your postcard will brand you daily and for an extended period of time. Not only do I find it to be a savvy business practice, I genuinely enjoy making someone's day with the simple task of sending a postcard. Do the same as you create amazing relationships in your territory.

Thank you Cards

Brand yourself in your thank you cards. When I first started selling, I didn't buy thank you cards. I took a Microsoft Word document and broke the page into three identical rectangles on portrait view. Each rectangle had my picture and company information in the upper left-hand corner. I went to a local print shop and had these printed on heavy paper. The result was a blank canvas marketing me that fit perfectly into a business envelope.

As another unique marketing approach, I found my face and company information often hanging up in the client's office. Branding does not have to be expensive. Each sheet of three, I manually cut with a paper cutter for a total cost of twenty-five cents. My eight-cent thank you cards were a good deal. This was another item that was not expensed through my company. I was investing in myself.

Pens

Marketing and branding is a constant reminder of you and your business. There are very few items that your prospects and clients will use every day that you can cheaply brand yourself on, but pens are one that I thoroughly enjoy.

Most people will always take a free pen even when they don't sign up with your company. On a custom order, you can have your name and cell phone number printed on a pen for about a quarter a pen. Brand yourself with your cell phone number, so they call you direct. Do not brand your company. If you go on ten appointments a week, this will cost you $2.50 per week. Keep in mind, one additional sale from a pen will typically pay for your entire investment.

Whether clients sign up or not from the constant reminder in their hand, I happily pay for marketing that provides me with the opportunity for someone to think about me each day. Being elite provides you with one thousand and one activities that may not provide you with immediate gratification. Your job is to follow the process and understand that fertilizing your lawn doesn't mean you immediately wake up to green grass the next day. Work hard to increase your activities that provide green grass into the extended future as well as today.

Business Cards

I love business cards. I always have them on me, and I'll hand them out to anyone. You never know who will take your business card or who they may pass it along to. As a result, almost everyone partakes in the business card game.

While I think the weakest form of advertising is to stick your business card on a bulletin board, I put a few of mine on every bulletin board I see that has other business cards on it. I then grab everyone else's business card that is hanging on the wall for a very specific reason: to call.

"Hi, this is _____. I'm reaching out because
(Your Name)
I saw your business card in _____.
(Business)
As it appears we run in the same circles, I thought it would be beneficial for us to meet and discuss each other's business. I'll be in the area on Thursday afternoon. I'd love to come by and see your business. Does one o'clock work for you?"

As you brand yourself, notice the other people in your territory branding themselves as well. They are prospective clients, networking partners, and additional contacts.

Email Marketing

Your email marketing should read as if it's coming from you as a personal note. Even if it's been copied and pasted, the personalization of your email and branding of yourself is what will get someone to actually read it. Taking it a step further is having a referral partner send an email on your behalf.

It was rather surprising to me how many people requested a free copy of my book—even before it was published. The request for a free copy was extremely exciting for me as it opened up a new area of obligatory marketing and branding for myself.

Some of you may have received an email from one of your friends or family members introducing my website and suggesting that you buy this book. While economics teaches us that there is no such thing as a free lunch, I believe there is no such thing as a free book. For my close networking contacts and business influencers, I have asked for their personal marketing in exchange for a free copy.

While I would be happy if they would send the email that follows to twenty people, I always set the bar at emailing fifty of their closest friends and family members with the following copy and paste into a personal email as they assist in the marketing and sales of this book. I am extremely appreciative to those who are willing to send it to more. And even more appreciative to those who personalize the message and then add my requested message:

> I do not send these emails often, because I refuse to spam my friends and family with something that I don't think they would be interested in. However, a good friend of mine recently published a book on how to become elite in sales. He uniquely incorporates his travel experiences in the country of Cyprus to explain sales concepts, the profession, and best practices to become successful. It is the first sales book that I've ever read that appeals to both people in the profession and those who just want to better understand sales and selling as a career. I never realized that sales was in everything we do and how important it is for everyone to understand these sales concepts.
>
> If you're looking for an awesome read, I encourage you to visit www.grassisbrowner.com and purchase the book. Enjoy the book and feel free to share the link with your family and friends. It really is a great read!

Let your friends, family, and networking partners work for you. When you have a great product or service that they also believe in, you have earned the right to ask for their help. I have never asked anyone to send the email until after they've read the book. And I only ask them to send it if they truly believe in the email they're sending out. The result is a grassroots effort in marketing my brand, and my book is a compounding equation of referrals.

Not only is the free copy an incentive that creates obligation to help me, the ability to provide social collateral to their friends and family provides intrinsic benefit as well. As we learned before, humans genuinely love to refer a product they believe will benefit someone else. It feels good to be the expert and share something with someone that they did not know about.

If you were referred by someone to read this book, please do me a small favor. Take the next thirty seconds to send a quick text message or an email thanking the person who referred you to this book. Let them know you are on chapter 13 and were instructed to do so, but the real reason you are sending the message is because you enjoyed _____ in this book. As long as you are enjoying the book, I thank you in advance for taking the next thirty seconds to do me this small favor. I really appreciate it and thank you for taking the time!

Have you started to pick up on where I practice the sales concepts throughout the book and explicitly explain how this book is in essence a sales pitch to you, the reader?

The Ice Cream Man

No one is more dedicated to branding themselves in their territory than the ice cream man. And I had no idea how dedicated these people were to making themselves known in the tourist beaches of Cyprus until I saw it myself. I know their song well, but absolutely dread hearing it as I know it will get stuck in my head.

Not only do these ice cream trucks blast their music as they travel around the neighborhoods, but they have huge, bold, and colorful designs all over the sides of their vehicles. While you would think this would be enough to attract the attention of children to run outside asking their parents for ice cream, I'll never forget the cries of one ice cream man dedicated to his sales numbers.

At least once a day, I would hear him come through my neighborhood in Protaras blaring his music. But if the music did not garner any customers, he would stop at Alex's house. Alex was one of his regular customers with kids that would buy from him on multiple occasions. And I only know this because he would shout, "Alex!" "Alex!" whenever Alex didn't come out to buy ice cream.

While he was attempting to brand his ice cream with a song that children would come running to, he also realized the direct approach of screaming Alex's name may get him an additional sale. While I didn't like this ice cream guy or Alex, I respected his dedication to branding himself in his territory as the screaming ice cream man.

"Brand Yourself Like an Ice Cream Man."

While I'm definitely not asking you to play music from your car for the world to hear or shout out your prospect's name in front of their business, we can take a lesson from the ice cream man. As you travel around, you are spending your gas and time traveling. Why not market yourself as you travel?

A car magnet or sticker with your information is extremely cheap. I like the magnet because it can go on and off as you choose when to perform your marketing as you travel. Your sales are all around you, and a car magnet on the door is a more subtle way to not scream Alex.

You'll soon find as you become well known in your territory that people will notice you driving around, which will grow your credibility and their comfort as someone who is a part of where they work and live. You'll brand yourself as someone local and someone they can trust.

There are multiple lessons to learn from the ice cream trucks of Cyprus as they are not just branding themselves in their territories, but they truly embrace ABS (always be selling) as they are always selling. However, the best lesson can be learned from my favorite ice cream man that I met in Cavo Greco.

Photis branded himself in a specific location each day. He was stationed at a swim stop in the blue lagoon area of Cavo Greco that I'd stopped to swim at momentarily after not being able to find my way to the highest cliff in the area. It was a refreshing break from the sun and my scooter, so I was rejuvenated to ask the ice cream man for directions as I exited the sea. I heard it had an amazing view and this was an area that I had not yet explored.

As soon as he knew I only wanted information, he told me I had to wait as he immediately helped the couple that had walked up behind me. This made me feel my first level of obligation that I should probably buy something.

After his sale with the couple, he then proceeded to give me directions to navigate my scooter to the top of this hill and the highest vantage point of the area. Immediately after earning the right by being extremely helpful with the information, he was very direct as he smiled big and told me to buy something. I laughed and said I didn't want anything primarily because I was wet, in my swimming trunks, and had no money on me. He then pointed to a coffee can that was labeled "Information 5€." We both laughed, but I was extremely impressed.

I, obviously, wasn't the first person to hit him up for information that did not generate a sale for him. As a result, he'd created a second layer of obligation in an effort to close people on buying something from him. I'm not sure if he knew

The Ice Cream Man

the elite habits he'd created in front of his ice cream truck, but he was now my new favorite sales representative on the island.

The next day, I drove back to his location in Cavo Greco at the end of the day. I was hoping that I could catch him while he wasn't busy, so we could talk. As I approached, he was closing up for the day. My timing was perfect.

He laughed as he must have remembered me from the day before as one of his many "customers" that just wanted to get information for free. However, this time he introduced himself as Photis and we shook hands. He was born and raised in the area and bought the ice cream truck five years ago as his current source of income.

I immediately purchased an ice cream cone and to his surprise put 5€ in his "information tips" can. He then asked me if he'd given me a map from the day before. He had not, and I was extremely curious.

He handed me a map that he had created and printed. The map had nine popular destinations that people typically asked him about for directions. One of the locations was where we were standing in front of blue lagoon with his ice cream truck. He went on to explain that he'd give the map to "paying customers" and used it to network with the local scooter and four-wheeler shops that send people in his direction. It turns out the map was his third layer of obligation that I had not experienced the day before.

As I had continually gone out of my direction in search of sales and sales concepts along my travels, my scooter led me back to one of the most talented salesmen that I had the pleasure of meeting on my travels. I excitedly talked to Photis for the next half hour as he packed up and prepared to go home for the day. He became a current client of mine as we met up for drinks that night and became friends during my time on the island. While I appreciated his information and directions, I had a greater appreciation for his sales skills and our newfound friendship.

Marketing is a concept that many understand but not everyone believes in. A pen, a thank you card, a magnet on your car, or even a map often show you no immediate reward. Elite representatives commit to elite actions and do not concern themselves with instant gratification.

Elite representatives are building something grand and victorious. While many people will never see the foundation or the initial building blocks, these elements are the most important part of the building. Marketing is one of our best examples of a chapter that elite representatives naturally do without questioning the process. Being elite means investing in yourself and knowing that you are a great investment!

Prior to moving on to the next chapter, please take a moment to list three marketing items you will commit to in order to brand yourself in your territory. And then hold yourself accountable to these activities (two of the four As). Remember, it is great to be creative. The ideas in this chapter are meant to help you think outside the box. Formulating ideas that more accurately fit your business and industry are encouraged as this is your investment in you.

Marketing Activities:

1. _____
2. _____
3. _____

14

ABN: Always Be Networking

By the time I had lived in Cyprus for two months, I was proud to call Cyprus my home. I took great pride when I shared places and gave directions to other travelers on the island to somewhere they had never been. It made me feel as if I were part of the island and knowledgeable about my home.

My friend Pascal told me that he believed I was a Cypriot. Pascal got to know me quite well because he worked every day in my office café.

I can tell this was a great compliment as he describes his definition as the word *friend*. Pascal believes that living and breathing together makes you one of their own. He told me that being a Cypriot is as much about your attitude as it is where you live and your way of life. It came across to me as one of the warmest and most inviting things that someone had said to me on an island that is well known to the rest of the world for being divided.

I talked to him at my office café for nearly an hour one morning. As they say on the island, "Siga. Siga." Things happen in time, slowly, slowly.

Just as it takes time to become elite. It had taken me a great deal of time to get to chapter 14 in this book and to cultivate my green grass on the island. I chose to put in the additional time commitment to have something I would be proud of rather than quickly spit out a book that may not be as beneficial to you, the reader.

Pascal and I were in deep discussion as I'd been to North Cyprus over the last two days, and he was very curious as to what I saw crossing to the other side of the island. I could write an entire book on the "Cyprus problem," but that is not why I came here.

However, the brief history lesson is that in July 1974, the Turkish army invaded Northern Cyprus taking over the northern half and declaring this area the Turkish Republic of Northern Cyprus. The division of the two sides of the island has carried on ever since.

During my time on the island, one could move freely back and forth through border control for those who wanted to visit both sides of the island. For me, it was apparent as to the differences when I crossed from side-to-side. It felt as if I were migrating to another country. There were typical checkpoints, different monetary forms, and different official languages, which all contributed to creating a unique look and feel for each side of the island.

My knowledge of the island, the history, and my presence there took time to develop. And like most things, my surrounding network provided me with additional insights that I would have never had if I were merely visiting the island.

When I crossed the border back to the south in Nicosia, my friend Athena met up with me for coffee and later brought me to her home for dinner with her family. Hearing the stories from Athena and her family provided me with all kinds of insight to their personal experiences and the history of the division from their family's perspective.

Our inner networks become so influential because not only do you share many experiences with them, but you also grow closer as you learn and understand each other's beliefs. It is quite common to have a strong set of shared beliefs as you grow closer with your inner network through shared experiences. Not only does this affect whom you choose to allow into your inner network, but this strengthens the obligation to refer those inside this circle.

The best way to describe my current inner network on the island would be for you to look at your own inner network in the city where you live. This network provides you with friends, family, coworkers, and individuals at your disposal for numerous activities and help, should you ever need it. In most respects, we do not create this inner network on purpose, with precision or a set agenda. An inner network is built over time relative to your environment and surroundings that you've placed yourself in.

Our inner networks provide us with advice on what to eat, what to do, how to act, our accents, our culture, our beliefs, and so on. You watch out for each other, take care of each other, and formulate emotions far greater than any business transaction. Your inner network in essence becomes your family and a part of who you are.

As I dined at the home of Athena's family, her mother, Maria, enthusiastically brought me additional bread and food as if I were one of their own. I was proud of the networking that had occurred to provide me with such an elite experience in a home almost eight thousand miles from my house in San Diego.

And now, my new network in Cyprus was no longer a random person telling me where to get off the bus. My new network brought family, joy, and happiness. As we ate, Athena's son, Alex, played the piano for me. He was eight years old and was magnificent to listen to. The house was filled with music, joy, and laughter.

Nicosia was an adventure on my own and an adventure in my new inner network. Back in Protaras, my network was far bigger than I had realized. Ival, my scooter salesman, had just had a baby girl. I was invited to his home for a party to celebrate the birth of his child. My inner network provided a happy form of obligation. I was obligated to attend his party, meet his child, and buy some fun clothes for his newborn daughter.

And upon returning to my office café, Michalis, Pascal, and I made plans to go out for a mezé the following week. A mezé is a traditional Cypriot meal where food and drink come to the table in abundance and are only available to be ordered for a minimum of two people.

While at the time, I was simply proud to be called a Cypriot by Pascal and excited for the Cypriot meal with my friends, I reflected upon the true meaning of Cypriot that he gave me. I realized that he was calling me part of his inner network. We were true friends and moving forward had a much closer relationship.

Professional networks will be necessary to the success of your becoming elite. The most elite professionals are able to create networks that blend into their personal lives as well.

Imagine how much more powerful your professional network becomes when it is also your personal network.

It truly becomes a choice. And finding the right people to network with and create your business family with should be a professional and personal responsibility. The best networking relationships that I ever had blurred into the personal. You end up with more cliff-jumping experiences. Your personal time becomes a choice to happily spend it with people who are part of your professional network. There is not a more powerful network than your inner network. And elite representatives choose to bring certain professional relationships into this network with full trust.

One of my close friends is among the selling elite that grasps this concept better than anyone. His genuine love of meeting new people and inclusive nature provide him with a personality that has made him the best-networked individual I have ever met.

Shevy Akason has been the number-one real estate agent for Evergreen Realty for seven straight years. He also manages the number-one team that he founded known as Everyday Luxury Group. While there are more than 1,200 agents competing for the top spot, Shevy starts each year with the foregone conclusion that he is the number-one agent. His "I am" statement is as factual as the sky is blue, and to those around him, they believe it as strongly as he does. However, when you talk to Shevy, you'll find that it's not the sales numbers he concentrates on.

Shevy concentrates on people. I conducted an interview with him, and I was able to gain additional insight into how he's concentrated on his network to result in more friendships and sales than he could have ever imagined. I learned Shevy is so systematic on his approach to growing his network that although he doesn't expect business, he believes that there is a possibility of business in every interaction he has. Therefore, growing his network and clientele is never unexpected.

When questioned on where Shevy networks, he responded, "Everyone needs housing, so every interaction I have with other people becomes part of my network. That doesn't mean I talk about real estate in every conversation. It's more about listening and forming true connections with people. People work with people that they know, like, and trust."

ABN

Shevy has his own belief for ABS, and he viewed it as ABN—always be networking. It didn't matter whether he was at the gym or riding his bike through a park. He knew and understood that not only was the next person he met a possible addition to his network, but they weren't someone he needed to pitch right away. Shevy was simply growing his friendships and presence in the community as his credibility and sales flourished.

ABN—always be networking.

While embracing his ABN philosophy, Shevy is the most inclusive person I know. Whether you are his newest client or simply someone he met on the bike path, he is quick to give out his personal cell phone and invite you to a family barbeque. He truly loves meeting and being around people.

Shevy's genuine fascination and curiosity to get to know people is what makes him so great at networking. His invitations into his inner network are genuine and enjoyable experiences. This allows him to welcome his new networking contacts into his family like someone else would welcome an old high school friend.

As I dove deeper into Shevy's elite ability to network, I learned that communication, people, and psychology are all interests of his. Each one of these interests helps support his passion and creation of his diverse inner network. He explains it eloquently. "There are many types of people, and every person thinks and communicates differently. It's important to me to recognize what type of person I'm communicating with, whether it be one of my team members, clients, friends, or even a random acquaintance as I go about my day-to-day."

He is consistently looking to create positive and productive interactions across everyone he encounters. His ability to be unbiased to the productivity of each conversation creates numerous and many accidental networking partners and friendships along the way.

Credibility is not created from friendship alone. It forms from the trust that is gained from the friendship and knowledge in the industry. Trust and knowledge are two things that Shevy never compromises on.

> "There is no substitute for education and experience."
>
> —Shevy Akason

Shevy continually attends trainings and seminars, reads about real estate on a daily basis, and invests his own money into real estate as well. In his own words, "There is no substitute for education and experience."

He attributes a large part of his success to investing in himself and his own growth in knowledge and expertise on the subject matter. He further recognizes this as a large differentiator between himself and most other real estate agents he competes against.

Toward the peak of the last bubble in 2007, many agents were still telling their prospects that real estate only goes up. Shevy's team was educating people and showing them the downside of buying real estate during this time. To further establish his credibility, his team created a fundamental value report based upon historic pricing data—not speculation—that helped their clients better understand the current position of the market cycle.

While his approach may seem counterintuitive to many sales representatives, his business immediately started to flourish in a down economy. Instead of pushing people into deals they may regret, he was educating his clients on the current market conditions. If the prospect still wanted to purchase, they were thankful to be working with a true business consultant that they could trust. Not only was Shevy earning the right for referrals, he was isolating himself as one of the most trusted and well-educated agents in California.

Trust builds friendships and expands networks. In Shevy's mind, he was simply concentrating on the people and doing the right thing. He wasn't concentrating on the sales. His approach to become elite focused on his ability to create an amazing network. As a result of not focusing on the immediate sales and trusting the process, he has developed one of the largest networks that I have ever seen as he truly represents many of the skills I've discussed in the previous chapters.

It is important to grow your networks the right way as you expand your inner network to include your professional network. It's also important that you build these additional friendships from the professional networks you belong to. While Shevy's industry often allows him to expand his network by playing basketball or riding his bike, this does not apply to everyone. Remember, you should target people who can appropriately fit into your personal and professional network aligning both friendship and profitability.

The best news about professional networking is there are many isolated events or groups that you can attend and join to grow your network. You should choose the ones you want to be a part of. It's important you choose those that you find of particular interest. The goal is to find like-minded people that you'll enjoy working with. If you want to go to the happy hour event, go. If you want to hear a speaker on local tax issues, go. If you want to go to a local fair or a sporting event, go. All of these types of business mixers are out there. Find the one that fits you best to start developing your professional network—and have fun doing it.

Networking Groups

I often hear of sales professionals joining a BNI or LeTip group because they've heard it will get them more business. BNI and LeTip are the two more recognizable professional and structured networking groups. However, I still caution you to do your homework before you pick which one you join.

These groups are typically a weekly commitment and there is also a financial commitment to joining. As a general practice, you should never join the first one you go to. Once again, you are looking for business partners that you can add to your inner network and become close friends with. Numbers never lie. I typically suggest only joining groups that have a minimum of twenty members. The more people in the group equates to more referrals and more opportunities of finding professional relationships that can become personal as well.

Once you've found a group you are interested in that has the right size, you need to interview the members of the group. Find out how much business is being passed among the members. Make sure there is positive energy and determine if you want to make the time commitment of coming to this group each week.

Many elite representatives know that the longest they will be in one of these groups is one year. This is more than enough time to formulate close relationships with the best members of the group. As a result, you are able to leave the group and continue to work with the members even when you're not in the group. Switching to another group after extracting the best relationships will compound the growth of your referral army.

Chamber of Commerce

I'm a big fan of chambers and the events they put on. These community events for local businesses provide the ideal opportunity to get involved in the community and network. There are some really fun events, and I see it as an opportunity to blend my personal life with my professional life.

I encourage you to bring your significant other to a Chamber event. But before you do, please have them understand your goal of meeting new people and networking at the event. This way they aren't offended as you hand out business cards like you are working on the strip in Las Vegas for a new club. To someone not in sales, handing out one or two business cards may be awkward. But it's a big part of networking and it's beneficial to have your significant other on your same team.

Whether you join the Chamber or not, everyone is able to attend their events if they've never been to a Chamber event before. People work with great people. Step 1 of earning the right needs to be present as you interact with everyone at the mixer. Go be awesome at the event and no one is going to care whether you are a member or not. After the event, you can decide on the profitability of becoming an official member.

But making relationships is how you get referrals; it's not by paying some fee and hoping the phone calls roll in. What you get from any networking group will be what you put in. Learn from Shevy with his "give first" mentality and while you shouldn't expect it, business will come full circle to you when you network the right way.

Power Partners

Power partners is a term coined in many networking circles. These would be people in particular industries that make sense for you to partner up with and send each other referrals in bulk as you grow the trust of your "power partner" relationship. Quite often, the easiest way to grow a power partner relationship is by being the first to refer. It will breed

"Giving to Your Power Partners Makes You Stronger."

trust and obligation as you start to work with someone who could be very influential to your business.

You should definitely know the people who make sense for you to be working with. You'll want to find people in these industries that you can bring into your inner network. But never discredit someone who isn't in a "power partner" position. Someone who understands sales and values your relationship along with what you bring to the table can provide you with more referrals than someone who is a great fit for you to network with.

Family

We learned from Shevy that bringing professional relationships into your inner network or family is the most powerful way to allow your networking to work for you. The best way to expand your inner network is through trust and credibility.

Shevy teaches us that these opportunities are present every day and everywhere we go. It is so much easier to call out your friends or family for business and referrals. Not only will it be comfortable and appropriate to ask because your friends and family believe in you and know you do a great job, but it will typically be understood without question. You won't have to ask because this group will feel the strongest obligation to refer and use you.

You'll find your inner network in your professional career brings you the most satisfaction and enjoyment. While many people don't regularly expand their circle of friends after their college years, you'll find that expanding this inner network will not only enrich your life but also expand and enrich the lives of those around you.

I felt extremely appreciative of my inner network in Cyprus. Not only had I made lifelong friends, but I had experiences on the island that were not possible without many of these amazing people. Concentrating on people often creates new and unique results both personal and professional.

As we continue our exercises to grow your business the right way, please list three professional contacts that you can bring into your inner network. Your next steps should include a birthday party, a sporting event, a family outing together, or whatever you deem as an activity to take the next step in developing your personal relationship.

Professional Contact and Personal Networking Event:

1. _____
2. _____
3. _____

_{Be specific and provide yourself with due dates to hold yourself accountable.}

15

Grow Your Author's Beard

My first residence in Cyprus was in Limassol. After that, I made my home on the east side of the island after I fell in love with my place in Protaras. After Protaras, I migrated over to Paralimni. I then moved to Ayia Napa, which is more popularly known to the tourists as the "party" area before returning back to my original home in Protaras. My little moves around the island forced me out of my comfort zone and created obligation for me to learn some of these areas better by living in them, not just visiting them.

By migrating around the island, it forced me into exploration. Many days the only exploration I had was taking a left on my scooter when I knew I should be taking a right. Not allowing myself to establish too many set routines accelerated the creative side of my mind and was stimulating for my writing. It's a concept that is continually being researched, but I don't argue with things that work. Exploring and traveling was positive for my writing and creativity.

The reality is that most humans function off routine and the comfort it provides. In my professional career, my routines and habits have created far more success than my creativity. Don't misinterpret this concept; creativity is an innate trait of nearly all elite sales representatives. And I do encourage you to be creative with all of your activity where you feel it can be improved and provide a more efficient process.

But as we've learned, one must show up each day with one thousand and one activities to make sure they are elite. It is impossible to creatively change and reinvent these new activities each and every day. This creates a bulk of the heavy lifting as established habits and routines. Once your elite activities become part of your normal day, you will have a hard time doing things any other way.

To test out this point with myself and my travels, I decided to experiment with my author's beard that I had grown out along the way. I hadn't been clean-shaven in nearly two months as I was "dressing the part." Uncomfortable at first, it grew comfortable on me and all the people around me only knew me with a beard.

One day, I shaved my entire beard off to challenge my current routine. As I looked in the mirror, I felt as if I barely recognized myself. My entire appearance from the previous two months changed in one quick shave.

I felt intimidated to see some of the people who had grown to be part of my inner network on the island. And, without surprise, the reactions of my inner Cyprus circle were similar to my own. It was more shock than anything as I listened to the many comments on how different I looked. I even had Pascal tell me I needed to grow it back right away. I laughed as I enjoyed the honesty of someone I now considered a close friend.

We become so used to seeing someone a certain way, there is a surprise and shock to showing up in a completely different way. So, in this instance, we can put the gauge of time to just under two months for establishing a new outward appearance that became an innate part of my life and the lives of the people around me.

It's an unusual example of establishing a habit, but most of my examples are unusual. You'll actually remember them better this way as I sell you on the concepts in this book. Engaging stories and repetition sells. Make both a part of your sales process. Your value propositions should be thrown on repeat through your presentation to establish the value of your product or service as factual with an understanding of why your prospect should buy.

"Grow Your Author's Beard."

Your goal as you formulate these new activities is to take your sales skills to an elite level that the rest of your office will expect to see on a day-to-day basis from you. You will have formulated your own "author's beard" that will shock everyone around you if you shave it off. And you won't, because you'll feel uncomfortable without it.

Establishing yourself as an elite sales representative not only becomes easier to maintain, but it also becomes an expectation of your peers and manager as they unconsciously hold you accountable to a higher standard. These expectations push your activity and hold you accountable to the activities required in order to maintain your "author's beard."

Timeline to Establish a Habit

My two-month beard timeline is important, because we're trying to gauge the timeline of establishing a new habit, routine, or expectation. This timeline has been widely debated by many psychologists. It was Dr. Maxwell Maltz who formulated his philosophy on habits being formed in twenty-one days through his book published in 1960 called Psycho-Cybernetics.

Dr. Maltz was a cosmetic surgeon who typically found it took patients twenty-one days to get used to their new appearance. He took these findings and explored them with his own ability to adapt, change, and establish new habits. From this concept and his book, the twenty-one-day myth was born.

Numerous studies have tested Dr. Maltz's hypothesis. The studies have pointed everywhere from sixty-six days to twenty-eight days and the list goes on. The reality is we are all very different individuals and there is no exact answer I can give you that will work for everyone who reads this book.

I can tell you that whether it takes thirty days or three hundred to formulate selling habits of the elite, it will take a lot of work. The exact definition of a habit is "an acquired behavior pattern regularly followed until it has become almost involuntary." As a result, habits do not form overnight.

This chapter addresses the fact that the exercises and activities of the previous chapters do not matter unless they become an almost involuntary part of your business. Yes, new and concentrated activity will provide you with additional sales. But it will only provide drastic change to your annual volume if you add this concentrated activity on a consistent and daily basis.

Chapter 1 taught us about initial yardwork taking roughly three months depending on your learning curve, company structure, and industry. While we learn in this chapter that timelines are somewhat irrelevant as everyone, their company, and industry are different, you can use three months in the professional sales setting as a guideline (not a rule) in your efforts to establish your elite selling habits and routines. The one thing that I can assure you is that if you practice them consistently, these habits—along with the efficiency of each one of them—get easier and more efficient every day.

Some of you may struggle to perform at a new level every day and find yourself occasionally taking a day off from new habits or routines. (This is often called a cheat day.) Failing once or twice during studies has had no measurable impact on the long-term formation of habits or routines. Therefore, stay the course.

Your path to forming your new activities into habits and routines is simply one day at a time. Once you are no longer thinking about the activities you've learned in this book and they become an almost involuntarily part of your daily selling routine, you've established yourself with the right activity moving forward. Remember, activity doesn't always breed immediate results. But if you concentrate on the activity with an awesome attitude, the sales will follow.

Form Your Most Important Habits First

While staying in Ayia Napa, I wandered around the Ayia Napa square and met an amazing artist, Penelope Constantinou. Penelope is a local Cypriot artist who was born in Nicosia and has become extremely well-known to the tourist and local community in Cyprus. She graduated from the Academy of the Fine Arts in Florence, Italy.

For the last ten years, Penelope accompanied her aging parents to Ayia Napa for the summer holiday. She started doing portraits in the square for fun, but continued after meeting many influential people, world travelers, and dedicated fans. Her work is second to none, and one portrait sold for 18,000€ at auction.

Penelope and I began talking about my travels, and, as I often do, I started to ask questions about her business. She has a gallery in Nicosia that displays her paintings and artwork. These are her more profitable pieces; the charcoal portraits that she creates in Ayia Napa provide more of an additional income. As she's earned the right over and over again with ecstatic clients in the square, I started to ask her about how she capitalizes on this for referrals and navigating these clients over to her gallery or website.

She laughed as she knew what I was getting at, and then we had a heart-to-heart on whether or not she enjoyed being in the square every night during high season. As much as it was enjoyable for her to be in the square, it had become harder to juggle being in the square along with maintaining the growth of her gallery in Nicosia. Her preference would be to grow her business in Nicosia, while having her Ayia Napa client base reach out directly, with improved marketing to generate more sales for her gallery and website.

We dove deeper into her marketing, and she was proud to respond yes when I asked her if she'd been collecting email addresses along the way. She showed me a book in which she assured me she had close to a thousand email addresses of happy clients written down that had purchased artwork from her.

On a larger scale, her entire database was over five thousand email addresses that she was currently not utilizing for any type of marketing. I smiled big and asked her one simple question: "Do you know what the most important task for your business is?" She nodded and said that it was the marketing.

Penelope was in a fortunate situation for someone who was successful by simply earning the right over and over again. But she had not formulated any marketing habits to capitalize on her hard work. We went on to discuss whether or not she could enter in one email address per day into her computer. How about five? Ten? Twenty? I told her that I would be happy with one, and I'd be holding her accountable to do so. Three days later, she'd started to input all of the email addresses, and the process of formulating the most important habit for her business began.

Once the email addresses were all entered, Penelope consistently added the new email addresses as she avoided this situation from ever happening again. Not only did the accountability push her to move forward with the marketing, but the pain of this project helped create the habit.

Establishing the habit moving forward was painless compared to what was required to get caught up on all the handwritten email addresses over the years. It was also extremely rewarding as she knew how important it was to her and the business.

Establishing habits is not only good for the business, it is good for you. It feels exhilarating to accomplish tasks easily and on a regular basis that are vital for your business and future sales. Remembering the pain of not having this established habit allowed Penelope to smile each day she only had to enter five or six email addresses from the night before.

Penelope became a vital part of my business. While there isn't a ton of artwork throughout this book, all of it was done by her. Each chapter has at least one drawing that makes many of the important concepts in this book come to life. I feel honored that they were all hand drawn by my favorite Cypriot artist.

In turn Penelope has become part of my inner network. We both refer to each other as family as opposed to business partners. She has a copy of my book displayed in her gallery, and she continues to recommend me to her family, friends, and customers. This "family network" is by far the best and most enjoyable way to network. Family always believes in you and passionately refers you to everyone they come into contact with.

Penelope is family for me, so please take a pause to view her website. Go to www.grassisbrowner.com and click the Art by Penelope link in the Cyprus Photo Gallery. Whether it be a gift for a family member, friend, wedding, birthday, or just for fun, I highly recommend Penelope for her lifelike portraits and amazing artwork. She happily ships anywhere in the world, and I can assure you having one of her pieces in your home will be beautiful and end up being quite the conversation piece.

It will be a fun and interesting story to tell your friends how you came into contact with a native Cypriot artist who was the illustrator of a sales book you read. While you discuss your painting purchase, please help me out as well and refer my book during your conversation on your new, favorite painting.

Habits are extremely important, but it is important to learn from Penelope because you won't be able to develop all one thousand and one habits right away. You should always know what the most important portion of your business is. If you are unsure where you need to focus your energy, you should discuss with your manager or mentor at their nearest availability. Once you know what it is, develop those habits first. And if you don't have a traveling author to hold you accountable, find someone who will.

Your new habits of the elite are vital to your success, but you will see success quicker if you develop the habits that have the highest return on investment first.

Developing the most important habits first is as equally important as taking a look at your current bad habits. Bad habits could be personal or professional, but they are habits that will get in the way of your becoming elite.

I decided to experience the night life in Ayia Napa with a few friends from my travels. I'm not much for loud music and drinking into the early hours of the morning. But it's a portion of the island that attracts thousands of tourists every year. As I barely set foot in the Ayia Napa night scene known as "Bar Street," I felt as if it would be a good adventure prior to leaving.

While drinking all night is light years away from becoming a habit for me, I was unproductive from all standpoints the next day. In fact, it took me two nights of good sleep to feel as if I was back to normal. It's important we recognize these types of isolated events or possibly consistent habits that we have created in our personal lives that detract from us becoming elite. It will be much harder to join the elite if you are going out every Tuesday night until four in the morning.

The following page is your sales physical. Just as it's important to get an annual physical from your doctor, it's vital you get your sales physical on a more frequent basis to transform your elite sales activities into routines.

By now you have itemized many activities and timelines throughout the book. You should have participated in numerous exercises, underlined best practices, and changed many of your thought processes along the way. Bookmark this page to have your sales physical three months from now and hold yourself accountable.

Feel free to share this with your manager or mentor to have an additional layer of accountability. While initially uncomfortable, Penelope was very thankful as I held her accountable to a vital habit being formed for her business.

Sales Physical _____
                   (Date 3 months from now)

1. What am I doing well?

2. What could I do better?

3. Write three action items to grow your sales skills.

16

Three, Two, One, Fun!

In life, we all have certain fears that seem to paralyze us. It may be a snake, a spider, or public speaking. For me, I have always been afraid of heights. To better detail my fear, I am not afraid of heights as much as I am afraid of falling.

I've had this fear since I was a small child climbing the stairs of the high dive at Island Park Pool in Fargo, North Dakota, where I grew up. I enjoy standing on the cliff, but going to the edge and looking down is not for me. The hair on the back of my neck stands up, and I get goose bumps running down my arms as I inevitably picture falling. Over and over again, we tell ourselves stories to rationalize these fears. And in reality, most of us never face our fears.

As part of my Cyprus experience, I was determined to face this fear. And I did with our sales concept of, "You jump, I jump." As the story reads, I was not the one blinking about the cliff-jumping experience.

I rationalized with myself that there was nothing to be afraid of. I am athletic enough to jump in the water and fully capable of swimming. If I were to come up with a reason for not jumping, it would simply be an excuse as an attempt to rationalize why I was compromising myself out of this new experience.

Being scared is a normal human emotion. However, I can still experience that emotion with a choice. I chose to jump anyway. My brain told me that the adrenaline rush and the sense of accomplishment would provide me with a new emotion. I would immediately be able to substitute my current emotional state of feeling scared with a new emotion of feeling proud and happy that I jumped. Not only was the experiment correct, I continued this experiment to find it diminished the initial fear.

As I continued to jump off more and more random cliffs in Cyprus, I became far less scared. And as a result, I became far less proud of the jumping experience. While at first, it was a video that needed to be immediately posted to Facebook, later it became a simple way to have fun and get in the water.

I took the Aphrodite boat cruise, which tours around the east side of the island and provides tourists with a lunch and a couple of stops to go swimming. And while everyone walked down the stairway of the boat to get in the water, I jumped in from the top of the boat despite the "no jumping" sign.

I shocked many of the other people on the boat. And I was now the guy leading the charge for scary jumps into the water. The drop was about 20 feet, but it felt intimidating to most of the people on the boat as you had to climb over a railing and stand on a one-foot ledge before jumping in.

A few people followed after I jumped, but many did not. I watched one Ukrainian woman stand on the ledge for what eventually amounted to thirty minutes. I know it was thirty minutes, because I was one of the people watching and encouraging her. At one point, I even climbed back onto the boat and got on the ledge with her offering to jump at the same time. Despite encouragement from everyone on the boat and myself, she ultimately climbed back over the railing and walked all the way down to swim.

The reality is everyone jumps alone. No one can make you do anything. The decision will ultimately be up to you. If you want to climb back over the railing, you can. You've been given the tools that you need to rationalize that the activities you've read in this book will make you more successful. I know with 100 percent certainty that you can come up with a number of reasons as to why you may not believe some of these sales concepts will work for you or why it's the wrong time in your life to do them.

> "If I wasn't getting married this summer, I would implement everything in this book."

> "I just had a child."

> "I'm working on establishing a better work-out routine and eating healthier."

> "I'll do it once I lose twenty pounds."

> "These concepts may work for someone else, but they won't work for me."

No matter what story you are telling yourself, each one of these stories is the same. Your story is not an exception to this rule. As a result, all of these excuses are better summarized in two words:

"I can't."

The reality is that you are not saying "I can't." Your actual statement is, "I don't want to." If you wanted to do it, you would do it despite the fear, hard work, or uncomfortableness of doing something new and foreign to what you are used to.

Immediately, get rid of "I can't." It will provide you with the greatest power statement in the book:

"I can!"

Trying to implement everything in this book right away will give you an "I can't" statement and a medical condition that I refer to as "action paralysis." You won't be able to move or do anything. Just pick one activity from this book that you are excited to implement and know that you can do it. It will be your first step on your path to becoming elite.

As I mentioned, I was able to jump with more and more confidence and less fear as I repeatedly faced my anxiety over heights. As I continued to jump along the way, it got easier and easier. In fact, I got to the point where I was able to push myself much further than I thought I could ever go.

My ice cream friend, Photis, introduced me one night to the owner of the bungee jumping place in Ayia Napa. We went after it closed, and I got to know Paz over a couple of drinks at his business. He was an amazing man who was well traveled, well educated, and well spoken. As we talked into the night, he let me know that he was going to head home but wanted me to come back the next day. He would be having an afternoon party at the business, and he wanted me to come back and jump at a substantially discounted rate.

I didn't know whether to thank Photis for helping my inner network expand with a new friend or run for my scooter and never come back. I've never bungee jumped before, and I've never been interested in having this experience at 200 feet in the air.

Not only could I selectively choose to not write about this invitation in the book, but I'd already faced my fears by jumping off so many cliffs and boats ranging from fifteen to nearly 50 feet high. As I provided myself with this excuse among almost a hundred others as I drove home on my scooter, I realized that my jumping had advanced to a new level that I could now achieve.

As we face our fears continually, we open ourselves up to new and even greater experiences that we didn't think were possible. Jump by jump, we are able to arrive at new challenges that we thought were unimaginable. However, with time, we believe they can be accomplished.

The next day, I drove my scooter to Napa Bungee and told the man at the entrance that I was friends with Paz. These were my instructions to enter for free upon my return. It worked as he pointed me in the direction of his boss by the bungee jump. Paz grinned from ear-to-ear and gave me a hug. He was happy I came back and even more excited that I was going to bungee jump for my first time at his place. He told Lisa to only charge me 20€ (US $25). With my hands shaking, I paid her and filled out my form. And to my surprise, they started to suit me up immediately.

How could this be happening so fast? I thought I'd at least have a moment to watch a couple of people jump, maybe get a drink, or just hang out for a bit. But, ultimately, waiting to jump would have led to the formulation of many excuses. Paz was coming to the top of the jumping platform with me along with one employee and one other jumper who was a regular at the park. His name was Marcus and he jumped every week. While this was no big deal for him, I was trying not to urinate on myself as the elevator reached the top of the structure.

The view was incredible as I took a couple of photographs on my phone. While I wanted to avoid looking down, I was determined to face my fears head on. On the top of Napa Bungee's roof read a sign: "Go jump. Just do it!" Paz had painted his own "I can" statement on the top of his roof to encourage each jumper to take the leap.

I was in, and I was committed. My trip was nearing an end and this seemed like a huge accomplishment to achieve prior to leaving my home in Cyprus.

As I hopped over to the ledge with my feet strapped tightly together, Paz gave me my instructions. "You're going to open your arms really wide, and I'm going to count three, two, one. When I get to one, you are going to fall forward."

I said, "Okay," without the enthusiasm I would have preferred as I write this. But at that moment, I was back to being afraid of heights. All I'm thinking about as I look down 200 feet is that the small inflatable square was only there to cradle the impact of my body for easier clean-up. And this statement is only true if I'm lucky enough to land on the square.

My emotions were in complete control of my current experience. I can tell you at the top of the bungee structure that I was not having a good time. Determined to alter my emotional state, I decided to move forward on something that felt completely unnatural and even more uncomfortable.

Paz began his countdown. "Three. Two. One. Fun!" I barely heard him yell the word fun as I was falling forward. While this entire experience provided me with an awkward and uncomfortable feeling, it also gave me the most rewarding leap in conquering my fear of heights. Not only was I proud to have made the jump, but it was also an extremely joyful experience to thank Paz for his encouragement while I accomplished this intimidating feat. I was extremely happy that I hadn't opted out of this new sense of pride by using one of my many excuses that were floating around in my head the night before.

"I can!"

You will take many jumps to form the habits and routines in this book. But doing so will take your sales career to the next level. I encourage you to jump as you will find a great sense of pride in growing your career one new skill and one jump at a time.

Transferring Elite Skills

Early on, we learned that tenure is an important and intricate part of becoming elite. However, I will now address tenure not being an excuse for your lack of success. Tenure is and always will be a contributing component to joining the ranks of the selling elite for the first time. However, there are individuals who achieve elite performance in their first year. And those who have achieved elite status often understand how to transfer their elite abilities when changing their company or position.

No one demonstrates their elite sales skills on a consistent basis better than my friend Todd Cassell. I worked with Todd at a Fortune 1000 company, where he always performed at an elite level. He was among the top ten sales representatives out of 1,000+ every single year, the number-one representative in the entire company seven times, and was ranked number two in the company when he left. He was one of fewer than ten people to sign up over 5,000 clients during his career with the company.

Todd recently took his talents to a competing Fortune 1000 company representing a similar product as a selling manager. His goal was to continue his elite selling skills and expand his passion for sales as both a mentor and a coach.

At the time of our interview, Todd had less than six months of tenure. "When I changed the company I worked for, I believed

> **"I always went out of my way to return phone calls regarding service issues, respond to emails, and simply take care of any issue that arose. That reputation has followed me and paid off a hundredfold in my sales career."**
>
> **—Todd Cassell**

that my referral partners and relationships would follow me. But now that it has been several months, it is more valid than I even imagined." Todd said this to my surprise. As one of the most optimistic people I know, he was even surprised by the results that he'd seen during the transition.

Todd went on to elaborate. "I always went out of my way to return phone calls regarding service issues, respond to emails, and simply take care of any issue that arose. That reputation has followed me and paid off a hundredfold in my sales career."

By continually earning the right, Todd's referral army had bought into him and not into the color of his jersey. Todd was once again working for an honest and ethical company, which was also important to his success. His former company was a great service that he was able to confidently sell and endorse for nearly twenty years. In order to protect the trust he'd earned with his referral army, his transition would require a continuity of joining another honest and credible company.

He let me know that this is the most important part of making any transition. "Having a company that I can stand behind and believe in their service and culture matters."

Without an honest and ethical product or service, there is no want or desire to refer the talented and elite sales representative. When was the last time you referred a bad restaurant? Probably never. No one likes to damage their own credibility.

As we dove into what drives him and makes him different, I discovered that his "I am" statement was something that he believed with passion. Like a professional athlete, Todd consistently concentrates on his goals and knows that he will achieve them. Making a transition to another company after nineteen years of elite success may be intimidating for someone other than Todd, but he already knew how the story would go before he'd even written his first chapter with the new company.

Todd describes that in order to be elite you must have specific, written, and clear goals. "I make it a habit to write them down daily. Putting them in present tense, with as much detail as possible." He goes on to recite the following as it appears he is reflecting on a past event. "Today is December 31st. I have successfully achieved the rookie of the year title along with securing the number-one position in the entire company."

While it was actually September 2nd, I did not consider him to be a psychic or a crazy person. I simply felt honored to be interviewing someone with such elite selling skills and practices as he shared his determination to never make excuses.

While Todd isn't psychic, he went on to receive the honor of rookie of the year for the entire company. In a short time, Todd was recognized throughout the organization as one of the selling elite.

Todd has a "dream board" in his home gym. It is a three foot by three foot cork board, and he cuts out pictures of cars, vacations, and other goals so he can see them every day. He believes in burning them into his subconscious to propel him forward.

He not only knows what motivates him, but he knows how to motivate himself. Todd's motto in life is, "Work hard. Play hard." While we've all heard this motto before and said it ourselves, Todd's awesome attitude makes sure that he has fun along the way. Remember, the shortest path to elite success is having fun. If you ever have a conversation with Todd, you will feel his energy, attitude, and charisma. His ability to have fun is contagious, and with a short conversation, you'll instantly know why so many people buy from Todd Cassell.

Being elite is not a box that you get to check and then relax. It is an ongoing dedication of fine-tuning your craft and staying on top of your game. Todd holds true to form as he explains his self-development and dedication to furthering his knowledge on business and sales.

While anyone passionate on elevating their career would love access to Todd's extensive library of sales books, CDs, DVDs, and assorted self-development material, he encourages you to start with one simple trick. Turn off the radio. During business hours, he uses the car stereo exclusively for motivational or educational material. Start your educational investment with a few CDs or sell your manager on buying you a couple, as everyone wins.

While we all have made excuses, we are able to alter the fear that comes with these excuses and jump into becoming elite. We learned from Todd that excuses are never a part of setting goals. As a result, he writes his goals every day and trains his brain to concentrate on his goals as if it is something that has already occurred.

While Todd's tenure among the elite is unprecedented, the tenure at his new company is currently not. Not only do we learn this is something that will not affect his goals, we find that even he was surprised at how successful he's been in his first six months. Prior to his first year of tenure, he was already breaking sales records to the surprise of many around his new company. By simply continuing on a path of earning the right with his prospects, referral partners, and relationships, Todd continued on his elite road that he'd started driving on twenty years ago.

As we move into our last chapter, it's time that you are honest about the fears and excuses you are telling yourself. Please take time to write your top three excuses as to why you can't move forward on implementing the activities in this book.

Top 3 Excuses:

1. _____
2. _____
3. _____

Now, make a big X through the words you noted and write "no excuses" over the entire exercise. I can bungee jump. Todd can transfer his elite skills to any honest and ethical product or service. And you can become an elite sales professional. Take the leap!

17

Your Grass Is Green

As I boarded my plane in the Larnaca airport, I handed my ticket to the associate at the gate who asked, "Where is your final destination?"

I replied, "Los Angeles, California," as it hit me that my entire world was about to change. I slowly took my steps to board the airplane. I couldn't help but think about how much location affects everything you do. My entire life over the last two months would have been vastly different had I been living somewhere else.

When you change your location, you effectively change who you interact with on a day-to-day basis, the food you eat, the clothes you wear, and the list goes on. We end up spending countless hours with the people we work with. Where your office or territory is creates your surroundings and location during the work day. The relationships you have with your peers and manager can end up being some of your closest friendships that you get to cultivate each day. This idea and concept brings me back to the introduction and the importance of growing your green grass right beneath you.

As they say in Cyprus, "Siga. Siga." (Slowly. Slowly.) It will take a lot of hard work and dedication for you to achieve elite success. As you start to implement what you've learned in this book, I reiterate that you need to have a product or service that is honest and ethical as you cultivate your grass. As you've seen throughout the book and through my elite professional examples, your ability to be honest is absolutely necessary for your reputation and credibility.

My grass became very green as a traveling author on a beautiful island. As the plane took off, I reflected with great gratitude and appreciation for the time I spent in Cyprus as my home. While I knew that sales was a part of everything we do, and it would be a big part of my travels, I had no idea how many amazing experiences and people I would have and meet along the way. Many of them didn't make it into this book, but I am thankful for every person I encountered during my travels.

I have been presenting my value propositions on joining the selling elite throughout the entire book. However, it is now important that I reiterate those values here. Think of the following paragraph like a proposal that you are walking your prospect through during the end of any sales presentation.

First, I want to reiterate that following the concepts in this book is a great deal for you and your family. You will effectively change your income level, increase your job security, provide yourself with numerous opportunities for different career paths and growth, become a leader and a mentor to many of your peers, and secure a new level of enjoyment as you achieve elite success in your position and the company.

The best news is that success only costs your time, energy, and strategic dedication to growing and getting better each and every day. This cost not only provides you with a ton of value, but it also prevents you from being part of the walking dead who never truly show up and achieve their full potential. I encourage you to move forward today on the transformation of your selling career.

I still understand that no one closes at 100 percent, and this will be no different for me as we conclude our time together. However, if I have sold you on implementing at least one of the concepts in this book into your daily routine, I will conclude with great gratitude that our time together was meaningful and beneficial to your career.

While my goal was that you would implement all of these practices and join the elite in your quest to seize the moment and effectively change your career, I celebrate each individual's growth and successful advancements along the way. Congratulations to you and the steps you've taken through the guidance of this book from your own hard work and efforts!

Your efforts do not stop here. Reading this book a second time will provide you with different insight from the first time you read it. Specifically, I'd suggest rereading your exercises and reviewing the notes that you've made to hold yourself accountable. As you continue your pursuit of becoming elite, your efforts should not be limited to this book or any other isolated resource. Your skills and knowledge need to be continuously fed to learn, grow, and get better every day.

Being elite means you operate in a much different manner than your peers. It is a choice that you will need to show up for. The reality is that, most of the time, the real story does not have a happily-ever-after ending. Most people do not choose to become elite and achieve their goals. They ultimately choose to ignore what needs to be done, because they don't want to do it. The task at hand is hard and will require additional work, time, effort, and commitment every day moving forward. The rewards are endless, but the decision to jump is always up to you.

Our discussions on human behavior throughout the book gave us a baseline understanding on the "why" to many of our interactions and activities during the sales process. You have also seen that, over time, psychological theories change and provide new insight and meaning to how the human mind functions and operates. Therefore, you should continue to commit yourself to treating sales as a science and consistently look for ways to improve on your best practices.

Being elite is an ongoing process, as I take great pride in the steps we've taken together along the way. Remember, the journey is just as important as the end result. Please make sure you are having fun with each step you take. Not only will it make your path more enjoyable, but having fun will provide the shortest path to success in sales.

Like anything in life, balance is important. My journey to Cyprus to become an author has concluded. Your journey to sales success is just beginning. I reflect on our journey together and thank you for your companionship during my travels. Remember, your grass is right beneath you and it can be as green as you want it to be. Water, fertilize, and grow your grass to be the greenest grass on the block. Best of luck to you on your travels as you journey to become part of the selling elite. Bon voyage!

Acknowledgments

I wrote this book to my grandfather in appreciation for his being a part of every step in my career. There were many forks in the road to lead me down this path, so thank you, Ken Markwardt, for always being a voice of reason with consistent advice and encouragement.

While my grandfather's encouragement often provided the conservative approach, my aunt consistently pushed me outside of my comfort zone to reinvent myself and do things my own way. Thank you, Lissa Markwardt, for your never-ending pursuit of encouraging me to follow my dreams. I admire your life coaching skills and your passion to help people in your relentless dedication to sharing your gifts.

To my uncle, Tom Markwardt, thank you for your encouraging words every step of the way. Your willingness to always go to bat for me does not go unnoticed.

To my mom and dad, Ron and Devonne Markwardt, thank you for your continual belief that I can achieve whatever I put my mind to. I appreciate you both cheering me on through this adventure.

Todd Cassell is one of the most elite sales representatives I have ever met. Thank you for allowing me to interview and feature you in this book. Your ability to achieve elite status each year regardless of the situation is what each reader of this book is striving for. Thank you for your friendship and sharing your insight.

Shevy Akason grew up three blocks away from my home in Fargo, North Dakota. The journeys and adventures over the years from Fargo to Southern California have only brought us closer. Thank you to you and your family for your love and support during this project. It could not have been more fitting for our careers to now blend together as I had the honor of interviewing you as one of two elite sales professionals featured in the book.

I can truly say that there may have never been a book without my original sales mentor, Tom Riley. Your kindness and insight to the industry have continually propelled me to pay it forward. Your friendship and contributions to this book reiterated your mentor role in my life.

A special thank you to Steve Weidman for recommending Cyprus as my destination to write this book. Your implementation of the sales concepts in this book with your organization was the greatest compliment you could provide me after reading the first copy.

To my publishing company and the entire team that worked tirelessly, thank you—Lisa, Sandy, Rachel, Ellie, Sarah, and all the others who played a role in creating a final product that I could be proud of.

Acknowledgments

To my many Cypriot friends and everyone that helped me along the way in Cyprus, thank you. Alex, Anastasia, Anna, Athena, Chris, Christina, Crina, Demetrios, Elena, Grahm, Joyce, Ivaylo, Katie, Kyriakos, Maria, Michalis, Oryan, Paschal, Paz, and Photis, each of you helped me bring my elite sales concepts to life on an island that became my home.

A special thank you to Penelope Constantinou. It was such a pleasure to meet you on my travels and have you become an important part of the book. Your sketches helped bring many of my sales concepts to life.

To the many individuals that contributed your time and efforts to help assist in the marketing and final production of this book, thank you. Special thanks to the following that went the extra mile with your help and support: Mike Benz, Shauna Bligh, Scott Engel, Travis Houston, Jamie Howard, April Kelly, Kelly Nettles, Nancy Markwardt, Kelsey McAtee, Michal Oprzadek, Jake Rodenbiker, and Dave Wyman.

To the many sales professionals that have worked with me and supported me on this adventure, thank you: Julian Ballesteros, Ryan Barlow, Tyler Bartholomew, Jorden Bastien, Mark Bottini, Erin Brown, Heather Calvin, Tony Capucille, Jason Chadwick, Angela Chang, Lawrence Chavez, Jason Close, Cristie Connors, Phil Coria, Crystal Cozad, John Craig, Jen Engel, Anna Evans, Cardedrick Foreman, Katrina Galvan, Brody Geist, Cliff Gibson, Kim Gibson, Kevin Godbout, Tom Hall, Parker Haney, Derek Hill, Kari Holden, Randy Holyfield, Del Humenik, Casey Ingram, Elizabeth Irizarry, Nick Jacobson, Miguel de Jesus, Laura Johnson, Angel Jones, Jay Kennel, Shawn Kravet, Henry Lam, Steve Lewis, Brad Lomax, MaryAnn Machado, Lois Makely, Jessica Marcinko, Erin Martin, Heather Massimo, Cindy Matalucci, John Matanguihan, Nik Mathews,

Chris McDonald, Steve McKenzie, Robert Means, Matt Miller, Scott Moore, Erek Newton, David O'Day, Travis Pederson, Amy Roberts, Lisa Robinson, Tom Roschek, Cesar Ruiz, Nathan Rutledge, Tina Sain, Bill Schuffenhauer, Troy Sherry, Hugo Silva, Pam Slater, David Soyck, Josh Stinson, Rhonda Teubner, Ryan Thorne, Courtney Tuggle, Walter Turek, Justin Volrath, Jason Wagg, Dan Westwood, Justin Wheeler, Mike Whelan, Jeffery Williams, Lisa Williams, Chris Witte, Jill Witte.

    I conclude my acknowledgments with an apology for those whose names were not placed in writing. I believe we get the opportunity to learn and grow from every person we interact with, so thank you to those who have helped shape and form my personal and professional career. You know who you are. Thank you!

About the Author

Jon Markwardt is a self-proclaimed traveling salesman. Literally. To write this book, he traveled across the world to Cyprus in search of proving his belief that sales is in everything we do and especially in traveling. Even his picture comes from his travels. Jon met a Cypriot artist that did this portrait and the sketches in the book. As an interesting  way to make some of his sales concepts come to life, all of the illustrations were produced along his journey.

Jon's work history includes selling and leadership positions for two Fortune 1000 companies along with building and scaling a sales, service, and business development rep division for a start-up company in Silicon Valley. His true passion is sharing sales practices through his writing and conducting motivational speaking seminars. As a result,

Jon was a featured speaker in numerous training capacities in all of the professional positions he's held. As a true believer in growth, he is continually advancing his own elite sales skills by attending advanced sales seminars, reading books on psychology, and getting in front of prospects to keep his sales skills sharp.

Jon is from North Dakota. He attended Augustana University and the University of San Diego. He lives in San Diego, California.

Another Book in the *Grass Is Browner* Series

Buy it today on Amazon.com!
Also available on Kindle.

GrassIsBrowner.com

www.ingramcontent.com/pod-product-compliance
Lightning Source LLC
Chambersburg PA
CBHW022055160426
43198CB00008B/236